The Torah Lifestyle:

Finding Meaning and Purpose in a World Transformed

The Torah Lifestyle:

Finding Meaning and Purpose in a World Transformed

RABBI B. SHAFIER

Frederick Fell Publishers, Inc.
2131 Hollywood Blvd. • Suite 305
Hollywood, Florida 33020
Phone: 954-925-5242 • Fax: 954-925-5244

Web Site: www.FellPub.com

Frederick Fell Publishers, Inc.
2131 Hollywood Boulevard, Suite 305
Hollywood, Florida 33020
954-925-5242
E-Mail: FellPub@aol.com
Visit our Web site at www.FellPub.com

Published by Frederick Fell Publishers, Inc., 2131 Hollywood, Blvd., Suite 305, Hollywood, Florida 33020.

Library of Congress Cataloging-in Publication Data

Shafier, Barry, 1960-
The Torah lifestyle : finding meaning and purpose in a world transformed / by Barry Shafier.
p. cm. --
ISBN 0-88391-044-6
1. Orthodox Judaism. 2. Judaism--Essence, genius, nature. 3. Jewish way of life. I. Title. II. Series.
BM565 .S44 2002
296. 7--dc21

2002004224

10 9 8 7 6 5 4 3 2 1

Interior Design: Lora Sindell Horton

Dedication

To my mother, Mrs. Isabel Shafier Z"L:

"All that I am, all that I will ever be, is because of you."

I would like to thank all of those who helped make this book a reality. To those who read the manuscript at different stages of its development. To my children, who had to put up with their father spending so much time away from them. To my dear wife, who supports me in all of my efforts and endeavors. To Phil Mulivor for his help and advice. Lastly, special thanks to my editor and friend, Rabbi Yoel Silverberg; the book is immeasurably improved because of your advice and input.

Table of Contents

Chapter 1: Introduction - What am I Doing Here?....................1
Chapter 2: David...3
Chapter 3: Appreciating our Wealth.......................................7
Chapter 4: Of course I'm Happy. Aren't I?..............................15
Chapter 5: The Voice Inside...25
Chapter 6: Loving Life and Killing Time...............................39
Chapter 7: God Blew It...47
Chapter 8: Who Are You?..55
Chapter 9: Purpose of it All...61
Chapter 10: "I" Am Not my Body...63
Chapter 11: Pleasure Without a Body...................................67
Chapter 12: Hello, This is my Funeral..................................73
Chapter 13: WYSIWYG- What you See Is What You Get............77
Chapter 14: Actors on the Stage...85
Chapter 15: Animal Soul / Spiritual Soul...............................97
Chapter 16: Pants Too Short Syndrome..................................109
Chapter 17: Torah From Sinai..117
Chapter 18: People Believe What They Want to Believe............129
Chapter 19: I never do Anything Wrong.................................145
Chapter 20: I'll Never Die...159
Chapter 21: Frank and Joe..173
Chapter 22: The Eternal People..185

Epilogue..199

Chapter I: Introduction

If you don't know where you are going,
it doesn't matter which road you take!

The Cheshire cat
—*Alice in Wonderland*

Little children are so curious. They are always asking, why? Why this, and why that? Why is the sky blue and why do ducks have webbed feet? Why is there sand on the beach? Why does a ball fall down and not up? Why? Why? Why?

Isn't it sad that when we grow up, we stop asking questions? It isn't so much that we know all of the answers, it's more that we lose hope of finding real answers, so we stop asking. In our school years we are trained to accept things, "*That's the way it is, that's the way it's always been, that's the way it's going to be, just accept it.*" After a while we realize that these are the types of answers that people around us are happy with, and we start to ask less and less, until we lose the ability to even question anymore. We even stop asking those questions that begot the pat answers. We become socialized into acceptance.

It's so unfortunate that we lose the instinctive desire to ask, the thirst to know why, because from questions comes knowledge, and from knowledge comes understanding.

The one "why" a thinking, intelligent, human being can never stop asking is, **why am I here?** I accept that God created the world. I know that God created the galaxies, the cosmos, and all that is contained in it. I also understand that God created me; but why? What is my purpose? What is it about? Why? Why? Why?

We human beings are a curious breed. We can go about life, busy as beavers, with plans and goals, five year goals, ten year goals. I will live here, get that job, marry that sort of person, send my children to that sort of school. Teach them these life lessons. We are so well worked out, so well planned, yet we don't have the foundation to it all. Why do it? Why pursue it? What is the purpose of it all?

Can I live without knowing the answer to this question? Isn't this the most basic and fundamental question that a human must answer? Forget philosophy, forget religion; one simple vital question that absolutely demands being asked, what am I doing here? Why did God create me? What is my purpose in life?

How can I get up in the morning and pursue a life's course without an answer to this question? How can I raise a family? What do I teach my children? This question is surely going to come up. It comes up in everything we do, in everything we value, and in everything we impart as life lessons to those we love. If I am alive, if I am a thinking, intelligent person, how can I continue without a solid answer to this most elementary question, **what is the purpose of my life?**

Chapter 2: David

It was a Tuesday afternoon, and I was sitting in my study when the phone rang, it was a voice that I hadn't heard in quite a while.

"Hi, Rabbi, this is David Goldstein. Do you remember me? I was in your Sunday morning class on Judaism."

It took me a moment to place the name—it had been quite some time. "Of course I remember you, David. How are you? What are you up to these days?"

There was a certain urgency in his voice when he said, "Well, Rabbi, that's the thing. I need to talk to you. Can I come over now?"

"Of course I would love to see you," I said. "Come on by."

It was a good thing that he had called before stopping by, I never would have recognized him. In my mind he was still 16 years old, wearing tattered jeans with rumpled hair. I still saw him back in our Sunday morning class: a bright, inquisitive young man, so full of life, with an impetuous vibrancy that was contagious. When he went off to school, we lost contact. The image in my mind didn't fit the person who walked in the door. In front of me stood a very handsome, impeccably dressed young man, in his early thirties; the picture of success.

I took his hand in both of mine, "David, come on in. It's been quite a while. Great to see you!"

I could tell by the look on his face that something was clearly bothering him. "Sit down, David. How have you been? It's been a long time."

"I'm fine," he replied. "Thanks for seeing me on such short notice."
"It's my pleasure," I said. "So tell me, David, what's on your mind?"

"Rabbi," he said, "do you remember in those Sunday morning classes how you would talk about our purpose in this world?"

"Of course, David."

"Well, Rabbi, you know I never told you this, but those classes really stayed with me. At the time maybe I was too young to really appreciate what you were driving at, but for the longest time I've been meaning to call you up and tell you that the message really had an impact on me."

David later explained to me that while he never actually put into practice what we had studied in those early morning classes, he always had a strong feeling that what we discussed was deeply and fundamentally true. In his heart, he knew, that one day he would return to it.

"David, I certainly appreciate hearing that, but somehow, I sense that there is something more pressing on your mind."

"Well, I kind of wanted to talk to you about that now. My purpose in life, what my ultimate goals are..."

I looked at David for a moment, taking in his still youthful enthusiasm, and said, "David, unfortunately I don't get to see you as often as I would like. Since you've moved away, we hardly get to talk. Of course you know that I would gladly talk to you about anything. But I feel I must ask why the sudden need to talk about this subject now?"

David turned to me, "Well, Rabbi, you see, it's this woman. I mean she's great. She is everything that I am looking for, we share so many things, I can really relate to her, and I respect her so much as a person. I feel that I have found the person that I am looking for."

"David, I am certainly happy for you. But, there seems to be some hesitation on your part. (In my heart I knew what was coming next. How many times have I been there, when a young man comes in and tells me that he has found his love, but she is from a different religion, and either his mother, brother, or uncle sends him to the Rabbi to get him to change his mind—I continued hesitantly, not wanting to hear the rest.) So what is the problem?"

"Well you see, she is kind of... well I mean in terms of religion, she is, um... how do I say this? She um, kind of comes from a different sort of upbringing than I do."

"In what sense?" I asked.

"Well, I mean she sort of believes in, I mean she practices..." his voice trailed off.

"David, if we hope to get anywhere, we must be open with each other."

"Well, Rabbi, she's Observant! You know, a practicing Jew. I mean she prays and keeps kosher. Every Saturday she goes to the synagogue, she doesn't drive, she doesn't turn on lights; the whole nine yards."

I had to admit, he caught me by surprise. This certainly wasn't what I was expecting. "David," I continued, "this certainly is an interesting situation. But what is the problem?"

"Rabbi, the problem is me. I mean, I am very interested in her, I could really see myself marrying her, but this religion thing, I mean Orthodox. It's just not for me. I consider myself a religious person, but how can I get involved in all of that; all those rules, commandments, and rituals. I've always prided myself on being a thinking person. How can I get involved in a religious system that makes no sense? Just blindly accepting things that I can't understand. It's such a different lifestyle. On the one hand it seems nice, and I guess had I been brought up that way, maybe it wouldn't seem so strange... *but... Rabbi, it's just not me!"*

"David, I have to tell you that I am happy for you. I have heard far worse things happening to young people looking to settle down."

I'm also happy, in one sense," David responded, "but my problem is what to do. I was hoping that you could help me sort this out."

"I'm always only too glad to do whatever I can to help," I said. "I hope that you can appreciate that this might take us some time."

"Rabbi, whatever it takes, I am prepared to invest."

"OK, David," I responded. "Let's get started."

Chapter 3: Appreciating our Wealth

"One of the great works on Jewish thought, *The Duties of the Heart*, gives a parable. Imagine a man who, at age 35, becomes blind. For the next ten years he does his best to reconstruct his life, but now without sight. Being a fighter, he struggles to create a productive life for himself. One day, his doctor informs him of an experimental procedure that, if successful, would enable him to see again. He is both frightened and exuberant. If it works, he regains his sight; if it fails, he might die.

"He gathers together his family to talk it over. After much debate he announces, *'I am going ahead with it.'* The operation is scheduled. The long awaited day arrives. Paralyzed with dread, he is wheeled towards the operating room. Given sedatives, he sleeps through the ten hour operation.

"When he wakes up, the first thought on his mind is to open his eyes. He prepares himself for the moment. He will now find out how he will spend the rest of his life. He gets ready. He musters up his courage and flexes his eyelids. They don't move! In a panic he cries out for the nurse. She calmly explains that the bandages won't come off for at least three more days. So he waits. Each moment is like a decade, each hour is like a lifetime. Finally it is time. With his family gathered around, with the doctors and nurses at his side, the surgeon begins removing the gauze. The first bandage is off, now the second. The surgeon says, *'Open your eyes.'* He does. And he sees!

"For the first time in ten years, he looks out and experiences the sights of this world—and he is struck by it all. Struck by the brilliance of colors and shapes; moved by the beauty and magnificence of all that is now in front of him. He looks out the window and sees a meadow, covered with beautiful green grass. He sees flowers in full bloom. He looks up and sees a clear blue sky. He sees people, faces, loved ones that have been only images in his mind—the sight of his own children that he hasn't seen in ten years. Tears well up in his eyes, as he speaks, *'Doctor. What can I say? What can I ever do to repay you for what you have given me! This magnificent gift of sight. Thank you.'*

"In Jewish Thought we are taught that this type of emotion, this extreme joy and sense of appreciation, is something that we should feel regularly. The feeling of elation this man felt when he regained his sight is something that we can feel on a daily basis, if we go through the process of training ourselves to feel it. We have this most precious, unparalleled gift called sight and it is something that we are supposed to stop and think about. Not once in a lifetime, not even once a year, but every day. A part of our spiritual growth is learning to appreciate the gifts that we have. One of the blessings, said in the morning, thanks God for this most wonderful gift of sight. It was designed to be said with an outpouring of emotion.

"We can have treasures for years, not once thinking of the wealth that we have been given, not once stopping to appreciate them. Not taking a moment to be thankful for them, until something happens, and we lose that gift. Then, it is Till then there wasn't a moment of reflection. Not one thank you. Not one word of appreciation. Not even a recognition of it being a gift. Now that it is gone the complaints find their home.

"Unfortunately, we don't take the time to think about the many gifts that we have. We become so accustomed to them that we almost don't know they exist until they are taken. How many times do we stop and appreciate that we have legs with which to walk, and hands with which to hold? How many mornings do we wake up and just take the time to recognize that we have our health and well being? How much richer is our life because we have eyes with which to see, fingers with which to feel, ears with which to hear, a tongue with which to taste, and a nose with which to smell?

"Each of these senses was created by God; created with much wisdom and forethought. Created for a specific intention, so that we should live a fuller, richer, more complete life—so that we should enjoy our stay on this planet. There is so much about this world that we live in that was custom designed, specifically for our enjoyment. But, it takes focusing and training to appreciate the riches we possess.

"To help do that, I would like to take a step back from life as we know it, a step back in time, to the very moment when God created the world. Picture, if *you* will, vast emptiness. Nothing. Absolute absence of anything.

"I remember when my daughter was six years old and we were discussing creation, there was one question that she couldn't come to terms with. *'Daddy,'* she said to me, *'I can understand that before God created the world there was nothing, not even light and dark, but what color was it?'*

"The difficulty that she was feeling was that we are so used to the world as it is, that the concept of *'before creation'* is difficult for us to fathom. The idea of the absence of anything; before there was a world, before there was even matter, space, or any substance to hold it in, is very difficult for us corporeal beings to deal with. We keep falling back to our way of viewing things in a physical setting, and absolute void has no place in our world.

"But, let's try for a moment to envision a vast empty nothingness. There is no space, no matter, there isn't even time, because time only exists in a physical world. Then creation begins out of nothing, because there is nothing. From nowhere, because there is no place; at this absolute first moment in time, God brings forth matter, the very building blocks of creation. Then darkness and light, not even separated, but intermingled—a patch of light here, a flash of darkness there. Next comes the heavens and the earth, the planets, the stars, the fish in the sea, the birds in the sky, and all of the animals of the earth; then on the final day at almost the last moment of creation, man.

"Every part of creation has to be thought out. There are no givens. There is no imitating or accepting the status quo, because before creation there is nothing to imitate or use as a model. Every part and every element of this world has to be thought of, planned, and designed from scratch. When we take this huge leap of understanding, I think we will see the abundance of goodness that God has bestowed upon the world.

"Let's start with something very basic—colors. The world that we live in is fantastically rich in color, with so many different gradations, shades, and hues.

"This is something that we take for granted. Of course there is color in the world, it was always there. But God created this thing that we call color and He put it in the world for a particular reason—so that we should enjoy sights. The world didn't have to be this way, if God was only concerned with functionality—creating a world that could be used—black and white would have sufficed. We would still be able to recognize everything, even shadows and depth, within the spectrum of the gray scale. If you remember watching black and white TV, it did a fine job, but it is lacking in a dimension, and so we don't enjoy it as much. God wants us to enjoy this world and so He created an entity called color.

"Look out on a fall day, and see the trees in their glory; the seemingly endless array of reds, oranges, and brilliant yellows, forming a magnificent tapestry stretching across the mountains. Look out at the sun as it sets, and you can see the most radiant show of color, the full spectrum of an artist's pallet, painted against a powdery gray backdrop. If the world was created for practical reasons only, all of the beauty that we witness wouldn't have to be. God put it all here, from magnificent floral scenes to exotic sea life. From the glory of the night sky, to the clear aqua green of the ocean. From a flower in bloom to the plumage of a jungle parrot; all of the pomp and ceremony of a sunrise—a world created in Technicolor®. Why create it that way? Why not make it all black and white? Keep it plain, keep it simple.

"The answer is for one reason—so that man should enjoy. God did all of this for us. So that we should look out at the world and enjoy its beauty.

"This is only one of the pleasures that we enjoy, but take for granted. What about food? Food is something that we need to maintain our energy levels and health. If its only function were nutrition and nothing more, then all the foods that we eat should taste like soggy cardboard. Yet they don't. There are so many different and varied types of foods, each with its own unique flavor, texture, and aroma. Why? Why not make it all taste like oatmeal? Again, for one reason, so that man should enjoy. So that eating, which we have to do, shouldn't be a chore but should be delightful. Taste is something that God added solely for our benefit—for our pleasure.

"An awful lot of thought went into creating the different foods that we eat. I once heard Rabbi Avigdor Miller describe an orange. He said, when you peel an orange, inside there are wedges. If you look closely, each of these wedges is surrounded by a thin membrane. When you pull back the membrane and look inside, you will see many tiny sacks. Inside each of those sacks is the juice of the orange. Why did God create an orange in that manner, with thousands of little sacks? The reason is simple, to further enhance our enjoyment. Did you ever see one of those children's candies, with a liquid center? They're advertised with the slogan *'Bite in for a burst of flavor.'* When you bite into an orange you also get a burst of flavor. Because the juice of the orange is contained within those many small sacks. When you bite into it, there is a release of juice in the form of a burst, and that adds to the enjoyment of eating the orange. God created those sacks so that there would be another dimension to our enjoyment. The sensation of eating an orange would be different without this feature. It still would have tasted delicious but this is an additional aspect that God wanted us to enjoy, so He designed an orange in this way.

"Do you ever wonder why apples are red on the outside?

"It is for the same reason that laundry detergents come packaged in bright colors. Proctor and Gamble® spent millions of dollars on research to determine which color has the greatest eye appeal. They have done countless studies proving that putting Tide® in a bright, neon orange container will result in more sales. Housewives like it better—it has more eye appeal—and therefore they will reach for it before the other detergents. Cheerios® has been in that same yellow box for forty years now! Studies show that that shade of yellow sells more boxes of cereal than any other color. People simply prefer it.

"So too, God made apples red, because it is nicer to look at, and that makes the process of eating an apple more enjoyable. As any chef knows, the presentation adds much to the enjoyment of the dish. So, God designed the foods that we eat, in a manner that gives them eye appeal, to enhance our experience of eating. Keep in mind, food is only needed to provide nourishment. Any other feature that we find is there because God had a specific reason for it; many of those were created simply so that we should have greater pleasure and enjoyment.

"Here is another example: What happens when you bite into an apple? You don't get that burst of flavor that you got when you bit into an orange. You get a crunch. Why is that? Why not design all fruits the same? The reason why an apple is crunchy is because it is fun to crunch on food. That's why your local supermarket has an entire aisle, 75 feet long, floor to ceiling, stocked with breakfast cereals, each one bragging to be crispier then the next. *"Crispy," "Crispier," "Crispiest" 'Ours is so crispy we even include ear plugs!'*

"Why is each food manufacturer trying to get you to think that their cereal is the most crispy? Because it is fun to bite into something crunchy, we like that sensation when we eat. So General Mills® makes their cereals crunchy—and when God made apples, He designed the cells to form hard walls, so that when we bite into it we get a texture that provides a crunch. It didn't have to be that way. God designed it that way, so that we should enjoy it.

"For the life of me, I still can't figure out why bananas are mushy! But, I guess that sometimes we are in the mood for a texture that is soft and squishy.

"What about aroma? Did you ever find yourself in a restaurant, and the waiter brought out your favorite dish? Your mouth was watering at the sight of it. But you had a cold, and when you began eating it, somehow it didn't taste right. You just couldn't enjoy it. Scientists now recognize that most of our sense of taste comes through smells. When God created food, He added this dimension of wonderful aromas to enhance our taste experience. Each of the different foods that we enjoy, not only have different tastes and textures, they all have markedly different smells, which contributes to our total enjoyment.

"Did you ever notice that when you peel an orange, as you break the outer skin, a fine mist of juice sprays up? The next time you peel one, pay attention and you will see that the skin has tiny bubbles in it. When they break open, they create that fine mist that emits the delicate aroma of an orange. Why did God go through all of the effort to design those tiny bubbles of juice in the skin? For one reason, so that when you peel an orange, you will smell its fragrance and hunger for it. When you hunger for food your enjoyment of it is increased.

"It wasn't enough that the flavor of the orange was made so special with a mix of sweetness and tang, and the wedges were made up of little sacks to provide that *'burst of flavor'*. Maybe we wouldn't be quite hungry enough, so God designed these tiny bubbles in the skin, to further increase our enjoyment. It didn't have to be that way. To get our daily dosage of vitamin C we could have done just a well without all of the enhancements. But God wanted to add pleasure to our eating.

"We were given many different and varied forms of food. From roast beef, to chicken and hot dogs. From avocados to yogurt, bananas, pickles, olives, strawberries and salmon; so many assorted spices, and flavors, all different and varied. If you look at a typical salad, you will see so many different shapes, textures, and flavors: tomatoes, cucumbers, green peppers, lettuce, mushrooms; each one distinct, each one contributing its unique qualities to the whole. Why? Why create them that way? Why not make them all brown like beans and taste like potatoes? The reason is because that wouldn't have been fun. The food we eat comes in so many assorted flavors and textures, each one appealing to a different element of our tastes. God preplanned and created all of this for us to enjoy.

"Yet how many times do we actually take the time to enjoy the foods that we eat? How much attention do we pay to taking pleasure from the sights that we see? It takes training and concentration to consciously choose to enjoy the life that we lead. If we do, we will see a tremendous amount of detail and concern that God put in for man to enjoy. We will see an amazing demonstration of the kindness that God shows to man."

"David looked up smiling, "I have to admit, that I have never focused on the amount of good that God put in this world for us to enjoy. I certainly see how thinking about these types of things helps a person live a richer, happier life."

"David," I said, "that brings me to an important point. May I ask you a question?"

"Sure."

"Are you happy?"

Chapter 4: Of course I'm happy, Aren't I?

"Am I happy?"

"Yes, are you happy?"

"I like to think that I am... " David responded. "I guess it depends on what you mean by happy."

"The reason that I ask that question," I said, "is that we live in times when there is an increased emphasis on having fun and being happy—on living life to its fullest. And, it seems that we have all that we need to do just that. After centuries of suffering, after a millennium of living in the dark, our society has finally found freedom from oppression and rights for all men. We live in an open and accepting culture and enjoy unprecedented prosperity. We have amazing health advances and live within safe borders; we no longer fear marauders or the black plague; we enjoy an advanced social structure and have technological wonders at our finger tips. We should now finally be happy.

"Yet, in my encounters with people, I don't find it to be true. I meet with a lot of people. And sure, everyone's initial response is *'Life is great, couldn't be better.'* But when you get past the social civilities there is a whole other world brewing inside. The truth is that most people that I counsel really aren't happy. When you sit them down to talk; when they come into my office and we get into what is really on their minds, I find that so many people just aren't happy. So many individuals who are financially secure, holding good jobs and important positions, people who enjoy great social acceptance and status, aren't happy—but why?

"We have so much. We enjoy so many luxuries and are so wealthy. It would seem that simply living in this generation we should be happy beyond description. We boast of greater prosperity today than any other generation that has inhabited this planet. Certainly, in terms of luxuries and comforts, we are unrivaled in the course of history. Yet we're not happy. I believe there is a root cause to this, and once we understand that root cause, we can retrain ourselves to enjoy life. But before we do that, I would like to focus for a minute on the abundance of wealth that we enjoy.

"My grandmother grew up in Poland before the first World War. She told me that her family was considered well off, they lived in a two room house. That meant two rooms. One for the parents, and one where the children slept, ate, played, did chores, cooked, bathed, and cleaned their clothes. That was it, two rooms. Period. And believe me, the rooms weren't large, and the families weren't small. Today, when we go on vacation and 'rough it' by putting the whole family, parents and two kids, in one motel room, it's cute and cozy—for an evening. But that was the amount of space that people lived in with all of their belongings, all the time. That was home. On floors made of dirt, with furniture consisting of the barest table and a few chairs, and wood-burning fireplaces that had to be stocked by chopping trees, this was how they lived. Walls filled with cracks that let the cold air of winter in, but held the sweltering heat of summer. Driving a horse to the market and bathing only on special occasions—without phones, TV, running water, or electricity—people lived. Regular people, our people, our grandparents, or great-grandparents, lived.

"We aren't any different than they were. They walked, ate, slept, and breathed as we do. They weren't born on a different planet, and they didn't live a thousand years ago. Yet their life was so different from ours that it is difficult for us to even imagine ourselves in that setting.

"I had a Tanta (great aunt) Perel who came over from Poland before my grandmother. When my grandmother first came to visit, Tanta Perel said to her, in an excited voice, *'You must see this. You won't believe your eyes! Our new building has a bathroom in the apartment itself!'* It was a standard of luxury that she couldn't even imagine.

"While it may sound like ancient history to us, it wasn't that long ago that people used an outhouse. In the freezing cold of winter they would don a coat, go out to the back, and there find a bare hut. This is how they lived. There was no such thing as cars, planes and buses. If you had somewhere to go, you got into a horse drawn wagon and bumped along a stone road for hours until your insides wanted to come out. Even smooth walls were something that was unheard of.

"Heat was a thing for the rich. My father had a friend who grew up in a cold part of Eastern Europe; he had a handy way of telling whether it was a cold morning. There is a Jewish custom to wash one's hands immediately upon waking in the morning. Many people leave a vessel, filled with water next to the bed, so they can wash as soon as they get up. In the early morning, before this man got out of bed, he would look in the vessel, if it had iced over he knew it was a cold day! I just want to remind you that water doesn't turn to ice at 58 degrees. And not at 48 either. He slept in the very room that the water froze in! Now we set our thermostats to a comfy 72, and if it goes below 62, we complain *'Hey, it's freezing in here!'* Did you ever have your furnace go out? You called the heating company, and they said they will have someone there by morning. When it got down into the 50's, you went to sleep at your neighbors. *'How could a person possibly survive in 50 degree temperature?'* Yet people did survive, people who were no different than you or I.

"We also enjoy material possessions that were unimaginable two generations ago. If you walk down an aisle in Wal-Mart®, everything you see is available to be had. In whatever color, shape, and texture you like, it is there for us to buy, and for the most part, we have money to buy it with.

"To give you an illustration, I gave a talk on this topic, and after the lecture a woman came over to tell me an incident. She was friendly with a new immigrant—a Russian woman. She took her adopted friend on their first outing to a large supermarket. When this Russian immigrant walked into the produce section and saw the abundance on display, she was so overcome with emotion that she fainted. In all of her years she had never seen so much food, so readily available. During the Communist regime it was considered a regular part of the day to wait for hours in line for food. Now, if we are held up for ten minutes at the checkout counter we are already looking for a new grocery store.

"Let me show you another example: If you own a house built before WWII, you will probably notice that no matter how large it is there never seems to be enough closet space. The home might have big rooms, plenty of bedrooms and lots of living space, but tiny, undersized closets. That is because the builders in those times built homes for the people who lived then. No one then would dream that we would own the amount of clothing that we do. I spoke to a woman who grew up in the 1930's, and she told me she had two dresses: one for weekdays and one for the Sabbath. That was considered normal.

"Now we have racks and racks of clothing: suits, shirts, slacks, sweaters, winter coats, summer jackets, light fall coats, ties, belts, pocket books, and matching accessories; not to mention shoes. My mentor, Rabbi A. H. Lebowitz grew up in America in the 1920's. When he wore a hole in the bottom of the one pair of shoes he owned, he didn't have the heart to ask his father for the twenty five cents that it cost to have new soles put on. So he figured out his own solution. He put a piece of cardboard inside the shoe, so his socks didn't rub out on the concrete when he walked. It worked well until one day he went outside and it was raining. He walked into a puddle—splash! His new soles were useless.

"Do we know of anyone today who doesn't own a number of pairs of shoes? In black, blue, and brown; ones for casual wear, ones for dress, ones for running, others for basketball, still others for bowling. Do you play golf? Of course, only an entirely separate wardrobe is fitting. And, heaven forefend to play tennis in basketball shoes!

"If we were to describe our wealth to people of a different generation, I don't think they would believe us. Kings in prior times didn't enjoy the luxuries that we do. If you look at pictures of King George, Monarch of England before the Revolutionary War, he was sitting on his throne in the comfort of his palace wearing layer upon layer of robes, topped off by a fur covering. Did you ever wonder why he was wearing all of those layers? The reason is because it was mighty cold in the king's quarters. The King of England with all of his wealth had to stay warm by huddling up to a smoky fireplace that heated up the part of his body that was facing it, but not the rest of him that was facing the other way. He still had to walk dimly lit, dank, hallways at night. He still had to sleep on a mattress of stuffed feathers. (Keep in mind, there were no chiropractors around to care for his aching back as he sunk down into 36 inches of duck feathers.) And when his brother, the Duke, was getting married, traveling to the wedding meant enduring a backbreaking carriage ride for the better part of a week. The Crown Jewels couldn't buy him the luxuries that we take for granted today.

"The reality is that we are wealthy beyond belief. We enjoy comforts and abundance that are historically unprecedented. And we aren't speaking about the captains of industry or the extremely affluent. The average taxpaying citizens of today live in opulence and splendor that previous generations couldn't even dream about.

"All of this doesn't even deal with the advances of technology that we enjoy. A colleague of mine was on a flight, and after touching down, the plane stopped at a distance from the terminal. The flight attendant announced there would be a slight delay as they waited for the walkway to be brought over. From out the window the passengers watched as a technician maneuvered the levers to direct a mobile gangplank into place. The person sitting next to my colleague remarked *"Look at the wonders of technology. They even have moving walk ways!"* My colleague was flabbergasted. Here they had just been traveling 500 miles an hour, at an altitude of 20,000 feet, nothing holding them up—no cables, no wires—flying in the air. And this person is astonished by a mobile gangplank! What happened to amazement over man taking flight? What happened to that sense of awe, that man has so mastered the laws of gravity that he can fly? But we are used to that. That was yesterday's news. And so we take it for granted. In reality the luxuries that we enjoy, due to technological advances are fantastic: From fax machines to e-mail, from packaged goods to microwaves, from cable TV to digital music.

"In short, we are wealthy beyond belief. We have riches that far, far exceed our needs. As a society, as a nation, as individuals we enjoy prosperity and abundance. We benefit from creature comforts that were unthinkable a generation ago. Everything is so readily available, so accessible; so easy. So I have one question, we have so much, are we now happy?

"For centuries, all that man has desired is freedom from tyranny, and a homeland where he enjoys liberty and rights. Armies went to war for this, entire generations sacrificed all that they had for this, and we now have it. We are here. We have finally arrived; living in a free society, with equal rights, and almost unlimited opportunity. Easily able to find sustenance, and enjoying unheard of wealth—we have it all. But as a society, as individuals, are we happy? Now that we are here, is it all that we thought it was going to be? Is this the dream that we were seeking?"

I let my words sink in for a while.

David responded, "You definitely have a point, we don't appreciate the wealth and luxuries that we enjoy. But, wouldn't you agree that, all in all, most people today are happier than their ancestors were in previous generations?"

"The truth is," I responded, "it is difficult to compare such an abstract concept as, how happy one generation is compared to another, but here is one barometer: Richard Earlstein, an economic historian with the University of Southern California, did an eye-opening study. He compared the relationship of increasing income to happiness. He found that, although the gross domestic product per capita in the U.S. has more than doubled in the past half century, there has been absolutely no improvement in the percentage of happy people. Which effectively means, that we have more than twice the goods available to each consumer, as compared to 50 years ago; twice as many cars, twice as many refrigerators, and twice as many homes, yet we aren't any happier. He goes on to say, 'Even though each generation has more than its predecessor, each generation wants more.' He points out something even more interesting: One of the most enduring cultural beliefs is that another 20% increase in our income would make us perfectly happy. But it just isn't true. Because no sooner do we get that 20% increase, that we need more, and we enter into this unending cycle.

"Do you remember the song from Fiddler On The Roof, "If I Were A Rich Man?"

"Wouldn't have to work much,
die, die, die, dee, dee deedle, dum
All day long I'd diedel deedle dum,
if I were a wealthy man."

"Even though it is hard to believe, there is still an inherent cultural belief that money will solve all problems. *'If only I were a millionaire—Wow, life would be great! All of my problems would disappear. I would be so happy.'* David, I am speaking about intelligent, thinking people, who somehow get caught up in this myth—in this never ending pursuit of wealth—all the while thinking, at least in the back of their mind, that more money means more happiness. But it doesn't work, because no sooner do they get more, then they need even more than that.

"Here is an interesting statistic: Within one year of winning a major lottery jackpot, 80% of the winners are back at work. Eighty percent! That means all of those people who for years were going on about how they *'Just can't wait to win the jackpot. Just one big one and I'm gone! You won't see my face in this joint again.'* Within a year they are back. Many at the same job they held before they won. How could that be? All that was lacking in their life was money. They knew that if they ever acquired some serious wealth, their life would be totally and com pletely different. Yet now they have it, and their life didn't magically change. They didn't, all of sudden, find this potion of unending joy and eternal bliss. Sure, for a while it was great; they couldn't believe their good fortune. But after they bought the Mercedes, after they traveled the world, now what? They went back to life, back to the routine, and they were the same person now, as they were before.

"You know, David, it is hard to find any real correlation between more money and greater happiness. And while we all know that, we live our lives as if it weren't true. We have been so socialized into this mindless acceptance of 'more money equals more happiness.' But it doesn't work. It falls short. It fails. It looks so tempting, so alluring, and it seems that it will fill all of our needs and wants. But at the end of the day, we are just as thirsty; not for more money or more luxuries, for something else—we just aren't satisfied.

"The question that we have to deal with is why? What is it? I have so much, why aren't I happy? I have a great job, a fantastic social life. I have unimaginable conveniences and luxuries. I have a home with straight walls and heat, with carpet in every room. Even my car is air-conditioned, so that I shouldn't suffer while I drive around on an air cushioned, suspension system. I own the finest sound system, and I won't settle for anything less then the highest quality CD recordings—it has to sound live. I have wealth and well being that is simply astounding. Yet I am not happy. But why not?

"What makes this question even more profound, is that God created a custom made world with so much thought and focus, all for my enjoyment. All of the beauty of creation: from the brilliance of a sunset, to the lushness of a tropical garden, all of the colors and hues are there so that I should benefit. All of the smells that we experience: from the gentle fragrance of a rose, to the aroma of prime rib, were put there for my benefit. All of the different colors, textures, and flavors of food all there for me to enjoy—yet I don't enjoy them. Why not? What is missing?

"What is missing is that all of these things only feed one part of me. Money and material possessions, honor and prestige, careers and promotions only feed one dimension of who I truly am. If man were a horse, then the formula for his happiness would be simple: Put him in a meadow, give him a bag of oats and a nice mare, and he would be happy. The problem is that man isn't merely a horse. There is a part of man that isn't satisfied, can't be satisfied with food and drink. There is a part of man that aspires far more out of life, and searches for significance and purpose. This part needs to live a life that matters and has consequence; it seeks out true meaning in life. Because of this, trying to make man happy by giving him more physical pleasure alone, just doesn't work. It can't work because it ignores one of the most basic needs of man. It is like drinking when you are hungry, for a while the feeling of being bloated subdues the hunger pangs, but within minutes the hunger returns, and now more intense than before.

"We live in very sophisticated times and it seems that we know all of the answers to mankind's problems. Yet it also seems as if we have forgotten some of the basics tenets of being human. It's almost as if we have lost some of the very underpinnings of life, and so, with all of our material gains, we just aren't happy. To regain that, we need a new level of understanding that begins with the most basic issues about being human: understanding the inner workings of the human personality."

I looked up and saw that it was dark outside. I realized that we had gotten lost in conversation. I didn't intend to spend so much time on this subject, but I feel pretty passionate about it. I turned to David, and said "Our work is going to take more then a few quick sessions. The issues that we need to deal with aren't about rituals or customs; they're about understanding man and his place in this universe. To do that we will need a strong understanding of why God put us on this planet, and what He wants from us. Even more, we will need to deal with the meaning of life itself.

"My suggestion would be that we make up a time each week to meet. Does Tuesday at 2:00 work out for you?"

"Sure, that's fine," David said as he stood up. "Rabbi, I want to thank you. I have a feeling that this is going to prove to be a very meaningful experience."

"I certainly hope so, David," I answered. "By the way, this young woman, what is her name?"

"Susan. Susan Katz," David responded.

"I hope one day to meet her."

"I would like that," David answered.

Chapter 5: The Voice Inside

When David came back the next week, I asked him if he had a chance to think about what we had discussed.

He answered, "I sure did. But while I admit that you have piqued my curiosity, I'm not sure I know where you are headed."

"In what sense?" I asked.

"Well, let's start with this: I find fascinating your observation that God added many features to this world so that we should enjoy our stay. I found myself thinking about some of your examples: I don't know if I can ever eat an orange the same way again! And I certainly agree that there has to be more to a person's life than only focusing on their own enjoyment. Yet, I'm not sure that I accept your premise, that unless a person finds meaning in their life, they can't be happy. In fact, I could see a person living a happier life not having to deal with these types of issues. Imagine a person who never has to deal with these kinds of questions like: What is the meaning of life? What is my purpose in the world? They would find life itself so much more enjoyable, just sort of taking it one day at time, dealing with life as it unfolds, unencumbered by any of these nagging issues. It seems that these questions themselves bring a person to be unhappy, and do not allow them to enjoy life."

I looked at David for a moment before responding. "On the surface it might seem so," I finally answered. "The problem is that God didn't design the human to function that way and when you try to use an object in a manner different than its intended purpose, it leads to disharmony. You see, God created us in a very specific manner, almost with an internal guiding system. If a person lives their life in accordance with that purpose, then they find peace, tranquility, and harmony. If they lead life at cross purposes with their inner self, they find themselves in discordance, because something is off. They aren't attuned to their internal compass, they aren't aligned with themselves, and as such, they can't be happy."

"Did God create us to be happy?" David asked.

"Whether God made us for that reason or not," I said, "a good barometer of whether a person's life is in balance is their state of happiness. If a person is truly happy, that is a sign that they are at peace with themselves, and the opposite is also true. Did you ever meet someone who was depressed for no reason; a person who had everything going for them, but lacked the will to go on? I have met many people who are successful at life, and they wake up one morning and just don't want to get out of bed. But the worst part is that they don't know why? So this person may seek help, they will go to their analyst or to their psychologist, and search for a solution. The real problem is that there is no problem. There is no apparent cause for their unhappiness. All systems are go, everything in their life is in place, and for all intents and purposes they should be happy. Yet they aren't."

"David, I would like to share something with you. For many people the reason that they are unhappy is because they are not in sync with themselves. There is a voice inside that doesn't let them rest—that isn't satisfied with the way they are living their life and that voice speaks up and unsettles their entire existence.

"David, Do you know what I mean by this Voice Inside?"

"Yes. Well sort of..."

"Let me show you what I am referring to. Have you ever heard of something called Jewish guilt?"

I got a chuckle out of David when he responded, "Sure have."

"While we tend to think of guilt as negative," I said, "it is something that is fundamental to our proper functioning. Let me show you what I mean. Have you ever had a nagging moral dilemma? Where you really wanted to do something but knew it was wrong? Not clearly wrong in the sense of a crime, more of something that we would call a white lie; something almost innocent sounding, but not quite.

"Picture this in your mind: Your firm is involved in a merger between two publicly traded major corporations. You are having lunch with an old school buddy, Bob, and the conversation turns to the merger. As it turns out he works for an investment firm.

'David,' He says. *'This is gold! I have a client who would pay a king's ransom for that kind of information, if you could just get me a few details, even the asking price and when it is going to happen, it would be so valuable!'*

'Wait, Bob, what do you mean?' You respond, *'That's confidential client information. What you're talking about is what they call insider trading. It's illegal, I could be disbarred. I mean people go to prison for that kind of thing. Forget it. No way.'*

"So you leave the restaurant with a kind of queasy feeling inside, not giving much thought to what happened.

"Later that day, the phone rings. It's Bob.

'Hey David.'

'Yeah, how are you doing?'

'Listen David, I spoke with my client. He told me that if I could get him that information, he would wire transfer forty thousand dollars into my account by tomorrow morning. What do you say old buddy, fifty fifty? Think about it, no risk; easy money. I'll call you later.' And he hangs up.

"As you hear him click off, you sense a sinking feeling in your stomach. Twenty thousand dollars sure could go a long way. As a lawyer you know full well: there is no way in the world that you could get caught for this kind of thing. One phone conversation, no records, no way to tie it back to you. Besides, it is too petty for anyone to get excited about. Just an easy twenty grand.

"And so the fight begins. That battle between two opposing forces, between what you want, and that Voice Inside that knows what is right.

'Come on now, who gets hurt?' You say to yourself, 'These are huge corporations; they have billions of dollars in assets. The only thing that is going to happen is that Bob's client will know about the merger so he will buy a block of stocks. It's not like we're dealing with some huge amount of money that will change the market... He makes out well, Bob and I make out well. No one gets hurt. Why not?'

"But that Voice Inside doesn't let you decide. It says. *'Come on, David, you know it's wrong. It's using information that you were trusted with, it's confidential for a reason. Besides, it violates the law.'*

'So what,' you respond, 'What's stolen? Where is the crime? It is just using some information that I happen to have.'

'David,' that voice says, *'it's against the law of the land. You took an oath to uphold that law. How can you go now and violate that law for your own interests?'* This goes on all night, this conversation between the two voices inside you. You barely sleep that night.

"Now, David, lets take this a step further. Let's imagine for a moment that our little episode doesn't have a Hollywood ending. Let's imagine you go through with the deal. The next day you call up your old buddy, a couple of brief sentences and it's done. True to his word within two hours twenty thousand dollars is deposited into your account.

"Now what? Initially you feel quite good. After all, that was the easiest money that you ever made. But at dinner that evening, you just don't feel quite yourself, something is bugging you.

"Susan looks at you and says, *'David, is everything OK?'*

'Yeah, just got something on my mind. Nothing big.'

'Do you want to talk about it?'

'No, just something I have to sort out.'

'You sure? You really don't look good.'

'No, no. I'm okay, really just something I need to work out. I'm okay, really.'

"That evening when you get home, you have little peace. That Voice Inside your head starts in.

'David, why did you do that? You don't lack money. You have a good job. You know why you did it: it was greed. Simple, plain old greed.'

'Oh come on now,' you answer, *'I'm thinking of getting married, twenty grand can go a long way towards a down payment on a house you know.'* But the voice doesn't stop.

'David,' it says, *'What's next? Cheating on taxes, maybe a little falsifying of documents, where does it end?'*

'Oh, come on now,' you answer back. *'It was a little innocent sharing of information, that's all.'*

'No it wasn't, David. How come you were so embarrassed when Susan asked you about it? How come you clammed right up? It's because it was wrong and you know it,' the voice continues.

'What's the big deal, no one was hurt, no harm was done,' you *shoot back.*

'Yeah, but David, it was wrong. You broke the law. Honestly, I'm disappointed in you.'

'Leave me alone!'

'No David, it was wrong and you know it! You did something that you shouldn't have.'

'So I did, so what? So I broke a law, who cares, people do things like that a thousand times a day.'

'Yeah, but David, you aren't like those people. You don't do those kinds of things. You should be ashamed of yourself.'

'Leave me alone! What are you my mother or something? Just bug off, and leave me alone!' you scream.

"The problem is that voice won't leave you alone. You can run from it. You can try to hide from it. You can try to distract yourself, but when you are alone, when your busy work is done, that voice comes back, and haunts you. And you can't escape it because that voice is you. It is that part of you that is embarrassed by what you have done. It is that part of you that is noble, good and proper. It is that part of you that only wants to do what is right. It is that part of you that strives for greatness."

Again, I let my words settle in for a while. Then I turned back and said, "David, when my children were young I got to see this 'Voice Inside' clearly. As adults we are very skilled at hiding our inner motives, even from ourselves, but little children are transparent. I can still remember when my oldest daughter was five years old, and she did something that

she wasn't supposed to. My wife would look at her and say. *'Sarah, did you take a cookie?'*

"Silence.

'Sarah, did you take a cookie from the cabinet?'

"Silence. Then a little voice would pipe up and say, *'No mommy, I didn't.'*

'Sarah, now look at me, and tell me, did you take a cookie?'

"Invariably Sarah would then look down, a look of embarrassment would come over her, a small smile would come across her face, and she would say, *'Yes, Mommy, I did.'*

"I want you to understand, at that moment, it was very important to this little girl to be able to say that she didn't take that cookie. She very much wanted to eat that cookie, and didn't want the consequences of having had taken it without permission. The simple solution to that problem was to lie. Just say *'No, mommy I didn't take it.'* She desperately wanted to say just that, but she couldn't. As much as she may have wanted to, there was a voice inside her that said, *'You did take it, you can't lie to Mommy.'*

"Children are innocent, and so that Voice Inside speaks out clearly. It tells them what is right and what is wrong. As we get older, something interesting happens. While that voice inside remains as potent as ever, we develop a counter voice that allows us to overpower that Voice Inside. When my daughter turned nine or ten she was able to lie. When that Voice Inside said, *'What you are saying isn't true,'* she was now stronger and was able to say, *'Just be quiet, I am in charge here, I know I took that cookie, but I am going to say that I didn't.'* At that age, when my wife would stare her down, there was no nervous sort of giggle that gave her away. She was capable of looking my wife in the eye, and saying, *'No I didn't do it."*

"David, don't get me wrong. I feel blessed to have wonderful children who are honest, and straight forward people. But there was a change.

"When they were young they almost didn't have a choice, they could be so easily flushed out. As they matured, they had to make a conscious choice to be honest, because they had acquired the ability to lie. They had acquired the ability to overpower that Voice Inside. Even though that inner tension was still there, they now had the capacity to act against that voice.

"We see the power of this voice in other situations. They aren't popular now, but there was a time when criminals were given lie detector tests. If you could picture a hardened criminal, a man who spent years making his living by lying, cheating, stealing, living a life of crime—clearly a person without a conscience. He is caught with incriminating evidence, but not quite enough to make a case. So they bring him into a room, hook him up to some monitors, and begin asking him a series of questions.

'How old are you? What is your name? Where were you born? Where do you live?' All the while a technician is noting the movement of a needle that is measuring his blood pressure. Then the questions turn.

'Have you ever committed a crime?'

'No.' The needle takes a sharp upswing.

'Have you ever been arrested?'

'No.' The needle shoots up further.

"When they get to that critical question, *'Were you on the scene of the crime on the 15th of December?'*

'No!' The needle all but jumps off the chart.

"Now let's understand what is happening here. We have a mature individual, who is fully aware that the information found out here will be used against him in a court of law. He recognizes the consequences, and he is also quite aware that when he comes into this room, he is going to be asked certain questions. He might very well have practiced the answers for days. Yet, when he answers those questions, there is a noticeable physiological reaction. He can lie to the court. He can lie to the District Attorney. He can even lie to himself, but there is that Voice Inside of him that knows the truth. When he answers what he knows to be a lie, there is an internal conflict that flares up when that voice says, *'You know full well that you stole that merchandise.'* Even as he is saying to himself, *'Just deny it, keep calm and tell them the story,' that Voice Inside says, 'But it's not true. I didn't happen that way.'* He may try to squelch it but that conflict is so strong that it has a physical effect on him, an effect so noticeable that a polygraph can measure the internal conflict.

"That 'Voice Inside' is something that we were given at birth; God created us with this inner sense of right and wrong, an inborn understanding of what is appropriate to do. When we do what is right, that voice lets us know it, and we feel good about ourselves. If we do something wrong that voice lets us know that as well.

"I am sure that you have heard of attorneys raising a defense based on their clients not knowing any better. I have read of cases of inner city teenagers being defended with a line of reasoning that went something like this: *'Since the time he was a little boy, violence has been a way of life for him. All that he has ever seen is the power of the gun. Since he came to any sense of the world, all that he has experienced is the law of the jungle: eat or be eaten. What can we expect from such a young man? Therefore, the court must have mercy.'*

"David, I consider myself a compassionate person, and I do feel for the plight of our youth raised in such intolerable circumstances. But, when a 15 year old pulls out a gun and shoots a man down in cold blood, because he wanted the fellow's leather jacket, the argument just doesn't cut it. You don't have to go to Harvard Divinity School to understand that stealing is wrong. You don't have to go to seminars about developing your spiritual dimension to know that murder, rape, and pillaging is evil.

"When God created man, He implanted into each human an inner sense of right and wrong, an ability to decide in each situation the correct course of behavior. That sense is this Voice Inside, this voice that speaks to us, and tells us the right way to act. We may be tempted to go against this voice, we may wish to ignore it, but that voice is there for all humans. Intuitively, without any outside influences, our youth understand that it is wrong to steal, rape, or murder. Just as the bird was created with an inner sense to find a worm, and the cat with an instinct to hunt for mice, man was given a higher instinct—that of right and wrong. The only question is, will he listen to it?

"This voice plays out in our inner self whether we want it or not. We may not have asked for it, we may not have requested it, but it is present deep within us.

"To show you what I mean, Henry Ford used to brag that he never did anything for anyone. He even prided himself on his consistency. The story is told that while walking with a friend, they heard yelps coming from a nearby field. A dog had gotten caught in a barbed wire fence and couldn't get itself out. Henry Ford walked over to the fence, gently pulled on the wire and freed the dog. When he returned to the road, his friend turned to him and said, *'I thought you were the guy who never did anything for anyone but himself.'* Henry Ford responded, *'That was for me. The dog's cries were hurting me.'*

"On the one hand, I think of this story as being an extreme example of selfishness. Where a person can become so self centered, that his soul shrivels up like a dried prune, but it also shows another aspect of the Voice Inside. Henry Ford didn't want to help anyone outside of himself, but he almost couldn't stop himself. He was pre-programmed to have mercy. In his inner makeup there was that voice that said, *'Henry, the poor animal is in pain, go do something.'* Even though he prided himself on selfishness he couldn't quell that Voice Inside. It truly bothered him to hear a creature in pain. The remarkable part is that this wasn't something that he trained himself in. It wasn't a sensitivity that he worked on. It wasn't even something that he considered meritorious. It was against his will. He was born that way. Implanted in him at birth was sensitivity to the pain of others. When he heard those cries, they reached down to his inner core, to that part of the human that only wants to do good, proper and noble things. There was a part of him that was touched, and bothered, that part saw an animal in pain and said, *'Don't just stand there, do something. That poor animal is suffering.'* He didn't ask for that voice. He might have even spent the better part of his adult life trying to squelch that voice—to deaden it, until it didn't bother him. But it was still there. When that helpless animal yelped in pain, it caused Henry Ford pain, and he had to react to his pain.

"That voice is part of us. No matter what level a person is on, no matter how far they have sunk, that voice is there, and it cries out to be heard. A person can spend their life desensitizing themselves, focusing only on their own agenda, ignoring anyone else in their relentless pursuit of self interest, but that voice is still within them. Sometimes buried deep, but ever present, and it emerges.

"It's an interesting phenomenon among people that good begets good. It is hard to quantify, but if you are driving to work in heavy traffic, and someone politely allows you to enter their lane, not only will the act of kindness touch you, but it will surface later in the day. You may forget about the incident, but there will be a residue that will show up later. Maybe when a secretary makes a careless mistake you will be unusually forgiving, or on the way home, you will allow someone else to get into your lane. It is a universal phenomenon that if we are treated with kindness we tend to (unconsciously) repeat an act of kindness ourselves. The reason behind this is that part of us; the inner spark has been touched. That part of us that is noble and good has been warmed and the result surfaces in our acting in a more noble, more humane manner. For this reason, even the most depraved person will react to kindness. Even the most barbaric killer still has that spark of humanism within him.

And when that part of him experiences true kindness it is touched and it reacts.

"David," I said, "what we call guilt is the manifestation of this voice, it is that feeling of discord that surfaces when I know that what I did really wasn't right. Granted, I may have desired it, part of me may have wanted it, but it wasn't right, it wasn't nice, and that Voice Inside tells me so, in no uncertain terms. We tend to look at feelings of guilt as negative things that we have to get past and grow beyond. We are told: *'Throw away your inhibitions, do your own thing.'* But God gave us that voice as our inner guide, as our moral compass. When we experience that feeling of discomfort, it is because we were hard wired at birth to do great things, and not live our lives to be self serving. By ignoring those feelings of discord, we are throwing away one of life's greatest teachers—one of the extraordinary tools that we were given to ensure our growth and development. That voice is actually a warning signal that goes off when we, the height of creation, act in a manner not befitting to our station. We may choose to ignore that sense of discord, to squelch that voice, but what we are then doing is throwing away our greatest moral guide. For man to reach the heights for which he was created, he was given that Voice Inside to guide him in life's choices.

"The true growth of a person is in developing that Voice Inside, and training himself to listen to it. Getting himself to the point where he is at peace with that voice. Until he and that voice are in harmony, traveling on the road to self perfection. It may not be easy, that voice is demanding. It demands that one be kind, that one do magnanimous deeds. It actually hungers to help others. It longs to be giving and compassionate, it yearns for real connections to other people—to be concerned for them, to look out for their welfare and well being. So it is a difficult taskmaster. But it is a master that drives the human to everything truly great.

"This Voice Inside goes even further—it screams out for meaning. It screams out to be involved in significant things, to accomplish, to create, to do things that will have an impact, to reach beyond the here and now. This is the part of me that demands a purpose, some higher direction in my life. It is the side of me that hungers for more out of life—more than just working to make a living—more than just getting up in the morning to make money, and then spending it. It isn't fulfilled with promotions at work, or a large portfolio of stocks and mutual funds. It yearns for so much more; it craves something so much deeper and more significant. It is the part of me that just can't be satisfied with the mundane activities of life; it needs something much more meaningful.

"This part of me demands a purpose in being; an aim, a direction, a mission in life. Without a clear purpose, I can't find satisfaction. I remain ever hungry, constantly searching. It won't let me rest when I occupy my life with frivolous and passing things. It cries out, *'What am I accomplishing? What contribution am I making? Is this why I was put on this planet?'*

"If this part of me isn't fulfilled, I can't enjoy life. All of the beauty, riches, and luxuries that I have, become meaningless. If this part of me isn't satisfied, it colors everything that I do, and nothing is much fun, because I remain, at my core, at my inner essence, unfulfilled, empty, thirsting for something that I just don't have.

"Now David, I am going to tell you something that may haunt you for the rest of your life.

"You can't run from that voice—that voice is you. It is there deep in you, it is part of your soul. You can spend the rest of your life trying to hide from it, trying to shut it off, but the voice won't stop speaking, and you will find no inner peace. You will find no tranquility because you are at odds with yourself.

"I can't tell you the number of people that I counsel who complain of not being fulfilled, of not having a purpose in their life. A woman may be a successful business person with an empire under her. She is at the top of her game, her company, highly profitable and growing, is poised for success. She comes to me saying she just doesn't see the redeeming purpose of it all. She can't find meaning in her life. David, what makes her feel that way? Why can't she just be happy? She is making lots of money doing what she likes. She is the boss, with nobody to tell her what to do. She certainly is the envy of so many people. She will say these exact words, *'Why can't I just be happy? I have everything, a great job, a gorgeous home in the suburbs, luxurious vacations. I have it all. Why aren't I happy?'*

"She is not happy because there is a Voice Inside that cries out for fulfillment. It cries out for its needs to be met. She has two choices, either listen to that voice, and in fact change her life—or suffer. I am sorry to say that many people that I meet choose the latter. They run—from interests to pursuits, from work to play, from distraction to distraction. Buy a boat, then a yacht. Watch TV, then a movie. Get involved in this project, then that. Anything, as long as they don't have to think, as long as they don't have to stop and answer, 'What am I doing? What is it all about?' I have seen people spend their entire life running to fill that void, but it never works. When they come back from Bermuda, when the party is over, that same emptiness is still there.

"David, you must understand this, you must come face to face with this one, cold hard fact: There is nothing here in the material world, no toys, no amount of money, no amount of honor or recognition that will fill that void. That Voice Inside is too real, it is too deep.

'Why aren't I happy? Why don't I feel fulfilled?' That we ask the question is as telling as the answer. It is because God created us for a destiny that is greater than simply getting on, making a living, going about this thing we call life. Because of this, I can't be satisfied with just passing time. I need more out of life. Not more money, or luxuries, or cars; more meaning, more substance, more significance. It is that part of me that says, *'I can't believe that God put me on this planet to be solely involved in the insignificant things that I do. There has to be more. There has to be a higher purpose. There has to be some meaning to it all. For heaven's sake what is it?'*

"David," I said, "why don't we stop here, and pick back up next week? Does this time work out for you?"

"Sure, it's fine," David said as he stood up, and walked to the door.

Chapter 6: Loving Life and Killing Time

We met again the following week.

"David," I said, "One of the things that we humans value above everything else is life. In fact, murder, the taking of a human life, is considered a cardinal sin of almost any moral code. Even in the most primitive societies, life is sacrosanct. A person doesn't need to be schooled in this—we have an inborn sense of the preciousness of a human life.

"To show you what I mean, picture in your mind an inner city hospital emergency room late on a Saturday night. The nurses are milling around, the doctors are lying on couches, coffee cups in hand; everyone is laid back, until the sound is heard: CODE. A man has been shot. The change in atmosphere is gripping; the place comes alive. The hustle, the moving, the focus, the energy. Once the ambulance pulls in, the level of intensity picks up even more, those once calm nurses are now scurrying like bees, the lounging doctors are now moving in overdrive. All energy focused, all attention turned, the totality of every being is riveted on that patient, now on the edge of life or death.

"David, let's analyze what is going on here. These are professional medical personnel doing something they do everyday. A man has been wheeled in with gunshot wounds. A man whom they never met before. A man, who based on the circumstances of the shooting, didn't end up here because he was an innocent bystander. A man, who is likely the cause of a lot of trouble to other people. Yet all of this activity, all of this energy and drive focused on saving his life.

"Why? What gets them so worked up? What gets these doctors and nurses electrified? They may be on two hours sleep, yet they are as energized and focused as they have ever been.

"You see, at that moment, it doesn't matter who they are, and it doesn't matter who this person lying there with the gunshot wounds is. There is one issue, and only one issue: A human life is at stake. A human life that will or will not continue—based on what they do. The gravity of the situation is enormous, the severity of the outcome is tremendous—and they all feel it. The doctors, the nurses, the security guard who escorted the patient in; the attendant who filled out the forms, they all are involved and mobilized in this grand and proper act, this holy endeavor, of saving a human life! No one needs to be reminded, no one needs to be sensitized, it is something that we all instinctively feel and understand: The supreme value of a human life.

"And yet, I'm not sure that we know why. While all involved intuitively realize the greatness of what they are doing, I don't believe that they could tell you what is so great about it. What is so important about a life? Why is it so precious? Why do we value it so? We may know it in our heart, and yet we don't understand why.

"Think about it, David, what wouldn't you give up to remain alive? Is there any amount of money that is too much to spend, to save your life? Is there any sum too large? And yet why? What am I doing with my life anyway? Here I am, I value life beyond anything else. My life, other people's lives, the life of a stranger in an emergency room, and yet, I don't even know why. I don't even know what I am supposed to be doing with it. I guess living. But what does that mean?

"This is one of those inconsistencies that we human beings are involved in all the time. Here's another example: How many times have you heard the expression "killing time?" Maybe you were at the airport and you heard the person in line next to you say, *'My plane doesn't take off for three hours so I have some time to kill.'* Or it might have been between semesters in school when you overheard some of the seniors saying, *'We have a ton of time to kill till next semester.'* Or maybe it was a friend of yours who was unemployed, and took up collecting bottle caps just to kill time.

"This expression actually tells a lot about our point of view: We don't value time. At best, we value some of the things we do with it. We certainly value people, things, and maybe even relationships. But time is something to be used for important things. If no important things are here right now, then there is nothing to do with this time that I have on my hands, so I might as well kill it.

"Now, I don't want to get philosophical, but what is life but time? What is our entire life, but minutes, hours, days, weeks, months, and years? We are on the face of this planet for a finite amount of time, and the ultimate measure of life is time. If we were very pragmatic about it we might even refer to life as *'How much time I have left? I am now 38; my mother lived to be 68, my Father to 93, where does that leave me?'* Meaning, *'how much time do I have left to live?'* I can't think of any more clear and obvious statement to make than, time is life. And yet, we flippantly speak about killing time, knowing full well that the very essence of what we so value, this thing called life, is only a limited amount of time.

"Now David, I want you to imagine for a moment that this very same fellow, who when unemployed, talked about killing months of time collecting bottle caps, is diagnosed with lung cancer. He is now in a battle for his life. The prognosis is grim. He reaches deep down inside himself and makes that monumental decision to fight. Whatever it takes, whatever pain he has to go through, he will do it. He has the emotional strength and determination to lick this thing. And fight he does. Going through months of treatments that leave him feeling even worse than the disease itself did. Spending days so weak that all he can do is lay in bed and blankly stare. He lives through four months of hell on this earth. Finally, he gets back the report: remission. They got it all! He will live!

"Let us imagine him the day that he is released from the hospital—A man with a new lease on life. A man who only a few weeks ago didn't know whether he would be here at all. He now sets out and plans his future. Can we assume that we are going to see the same person? Can we assume that his view of life is going to be the same as before he got sick?

"On his first walk out onto the hospital grounds, he is high. The birds are singing, the first smells of spring are in the air. The gentle humming coming from the fields, the forming of buds, and the fullness of the aromas that surround him, all fill him with an inner joy that he never experienced before—the sheer pleasure of being alive. Can we imagine a greater sense of supreme well-being? Can we imagine a richer person? His bitter bread tastes like the greatest feast for a king. Such a man is exalted; with his body on the ground, his mind among the angels. Such bliss.

"But now what? He now has a fabulous appreciation of the value of life. In the core of his being, he understands the opportunity of actually waking up in the morning feeling energetic and well. But now what should he do? Now that he has a new lease on life, now that he can really value each moment, and is ready to live life to its fullest, what should he use this priceless commodity called life for?

"You see, David, we are all in this dilemma, we all have this very deeply rooted sense of the value of life, and yet we spend most of our life asleep to this ultimate question: What should I be doing with this priceless commodity called life? And so we go on in this complete state of contradiction, all the while talking about the value of life, and yet so flippantly talking about killing time. We love life and we kill time, yet life is nothing but time!

"But what happens when I wake up? What happens when I come out of my slumber and come face to face with that reality that life is precious beyond words, but I just don't know why? What happens when I understand to the depth of my being that time is the most precious, limited resource on the face of this planet, but I just don't have a clue as to what I should be doing with it?

"There is an observation in the Talmud that makes this dilemma even deeper: If God's intention was to create a human race, why did He begin with one man and one woman? Why not create an entire civilization, or at least an entire nation? The Talmud answers this question by saying that God chose to create a single man and woman first to teach us a fundamental lesson: That it was fit to create an entire world for one person. So that all human beings throughout the span of time should look at themselves and say, it was fit for God to create an entire universe, and all that it contains, for a single man. I, too, am a man; therefore, it was fitting for God to have created everything, all that I see, for me alone. The Talmud even goes a step further. It uses the word 'obligated.' As in, 'Man is obligated to say that it was fitting and proper for God to have created an entire world for me alone.'

"This concept is so basic to man's proper functioning that it couldn't have been taught in a book. It had to be something that a person would come to as an understanding from studying the world. It had to be something that a person would look at and feel; that all of this, the heavens and earth, the moon, the sun, and stars, the mountains and streams, from the birds in the sky to the monkeys swinging from the trees, all of this was created for me.

"I find this concept heady. If a person looks out at this world in all of its beauty and glory, from continent to continent, from galaxy to galaxy, from the most simple life form to the most complex; the rivers, the oceans, the trees and the animals; from the African Rain forest to the Sahara Desert, all of this magnificent world, was fitting and proper to have been created for me. For little me.

"Everything that we may read, everything that we may intuitively feel about the importance of a single life, is true. It is true because that is the value of one life. The Talmud teaches us that if one saves a life, it is as if they have saved an entire world, because God felt it fit to create an entire world for that one person.

"But this only further deepens our problem: Why? We instinctively feel it; the Talmud strengthens our understanding of the value, the importance of one human life. But why is it so important? What for? What could one person do that is possibly so significant that it was worth creating a whole world for him alone?

"I want to share with you possibly the greatest story I have ever heard about the sanctity of time. Rabbi Avrohom Grodzinski, one of the great Jewish Leaders in Pre WWII Europe, was hospitalized during the Nazi occupation. His students came to visit him with grave news. They had gotten word that the Nazis were planning to burn down the hospital that he was now in. His students urged him to leave immediately. He thought for a moment and said. *'I am too sickly to be transported. In my current state, I will not survive. Evacuate whoever you can and then move me to the top floor.'* His students couldn't argue with their revered teacher, he knew his condition better then they did. However, they asked, *'What good will it do to move you further up?'* Rabbi Grodzinski answered, *'When they burn the building the fire will hit the top floors last and so I will have a few more moments of life.'*

"David, when I heard that story, I was humbled. Such a respect for life. Such an appreciation of but a few more minutes of living. But time for what? I see that life is precious. I understand that there must be some great purpose to it. I know it instinctively, in my heart. But why? I realize that my life, which I so value, is nothing but time. But time to do what?

"And this is the dilemma that we find ourselves in; we intuitively feel the value of life, yet we speak about killing time. We value human life beyond anything else, yet we don't know why. We read the Talmud telling us the extraordinary value of one human life, but based on my understanding of what we are here to do, and my current perception of the purpose of man on this planet, there is nothing that could possibly warrant creating an entire world for just him. There is something missing in my understanding of man and his purpose on this planet.

"There is obviously something going on here, something that is bigger than what I have been dealing with up until now, something far more significant and important, there is a part of the equation that I am missing, but for heavens sake, what is it?"

I turned to David and said, "Do you mind if we break off at this point?"

"Rabbi, do you mean that you are going to leave me in suspense till next week?"

"Actually, David," I said. "I think that this is some good food for thought. So why don't we pick back up at this point next week."

Chapter 7: God blew It

"David," I said, "I would like to make an observation: if we look at the world around us, there sure does seem to be a lot of senseless suffering and pain. So many bad things seem to happen: people get sick and die, businesses go bankrupt, there are earthquakes, floods, hurricanes, tornados, and car crashes. People break bones and lose limbs. There is cancer, emphysema, diabetes and shingles. There is hunger and famine in the world. There are broken homes and divorce. Then there is war!

"The worst part is that it all seems so arbitrary. All of the catastrophes that we read about seem to strike without rhyme or reason. A young man, on the way to his wedding, is hit by a truck and instantly dies. A 12 year old girl is burnt to death when the boiler blows up in the basement; a six year old contracts leukemia. And we ask why? Why do these things have to happen? Why all the needless suffering? If pain and suffering were meted out to the wicked only, we might understand it, but it happens to good people; regular people, people who are just like you and me. So, the question is why? Why would a kind and justly God allow these things to happen? Why would a loving God sit back while so much evil is being perpetrated?

"Before we begin the journey to answer this ultimate question of life, I would like to deepen it.

"The Talmud tells us that the order of creation was: first God created matter, the very building blocks of creation. Then darkness and light. Next came the heavens and earth, the planets and stars, the fish in the sea, the birds in the sky, and all of the animals of the earth. Then on the final day, at almost the last moment of creation, man. The reason that God waited till the rest of creation was complete, before bringing forth man, is because the purpose of creation is man. Much like when one invites a guest. First the host prepares the meal, sets the table, and arranges the settings, all in anticipation of his guest. Only when all has been prepared, is it appropriate for the guest to be welcomed in. So too, was it with man. The entire world and all that it contains was created to be used by man. It is his world. So it was only proper that all should be arranged prior to his coming into the world. So, man was last not because he is least important; quite the opposite, because he is the purpose and the focus of it all.

"Now, David, that being said, it sure does seem that God blew it."

"God blew it?!" David asked.

"Yes, God blew it. If it is true that God is loving and kind, if it is true that God loves all of his creations, then it sure does seem that God could have done a better job at creating this world, and especially man. In fact, it seems that there is much good in this world that God intentionally held back from man.

"Let's start with the animal kingdom, there are many gifts that animals enjoy that man doesn't. If in fact, man is the highest order of creation, wouldn't it make sense to take all of the strengths of the animal kingdom and invest them in man? Yet that isn't what we see.

"To give you an example: there was once a Karate Master named George Dillman. While George may have been a highly proficient martial artist, he had one flaw: he took himself seriously—maybe a tad too seriously. You see, George decided that he was going to put on the ultimate Karate demonstration. He had gone through the whole gamut of breaking things, first boards, then bricks, and then large blocks of ice, now he was looking to do something really spectacular. He decided that he was going to fight a bear. So he hired a circus bear for the performance. This bear had been trained to wrestle, and George got together with the bear's trainer to choreograph a fight scene between 'man and beast'. Of course, it was only to be a show. However, there was one problem: George decided that he was going to make headlines. Instead of just going through the fight scene as planned, he was going to actually knock the bear out.

"The day of the demonstration with the crowd gathered, George and the bear square off; the bear swings wide, and George hauls off and smashes the bear full force in the chest. Needless to say, George didn't knock the bear out, but he did manage to get the bear angry. Real angry! So angry that if it weren't for the bear's trainer, somehow stepping in and calming the bear down, George would have been killed.

"George learned an important lesson that day: you can be a high ranking Karate master, with 20 years of combat experience, but you can't fight against 600 pounds of solid muscle! It doesn't work, because a bear is much stronger than a man.

"So, I would like to ask you one very simple question: why didn't God create us like a bear? Why didn't God make man, big and strong, and made out of 600 pounds of solid muscle? Wouldn't it have prevented an awful lot of suffering over the years? Wouldn't man's stay on this planet have been more pleasant? Have you ever stood on a freezing February morning, waiting for a bus? No matter how many layers of clothing you had on, you still shivered to the bone. You won't find that happening to a polar bear. In the middle of winter they break open the ice, and go in for a nice dip. Why? Because the layer of blubber under their skin keeps them warm. So why didn't God make us that way? Why not create us just like a polar bear, big and strong, with a thick fur coat, so that we don't suffer from the cold?"

"That wouldn't be man," David responded. "That would be just a different type of animal."

"No," I said, "I mean take the same essence of man. The same personality, the same intelligence all of the features of man and put him in a stronger, more powerful body? Why not? Wouldn't man have been better off for the change?

"Let me give you another example: have you ever found yourself in the dentist's chair in excruciating pain? The next time you find yourself there, I want you to think of the Shark. Why a Shark? Because that mighty hunter of the sea has up to 25 rows of teeth, one set behind the next; if one tooth gets damaged another one simply falls into place. A shark is born with a lifetime supply of teeth. Now wouldn't it have been more convenient to create man that way, with many rows of teeth? If one goes bad, just pop it out, and in comes the next one.

"Why didn't God create man that way?

"In fact, we could probably think of many advantages that creatures of the wild have, yet man was not given them. He was created as is: weak, susceptible to attack, and subjected to the elements. It seems as if man was purposely created in this independent yet dependent mode. As if he was to be the master of his fate, yet still so fragile and vulnerable.

"An even clearer example of this is disease and illness. The same God who created a stupefying immune system in man—ready to pounce on every imaginable germ—also left huge gaping holes in that defense system. Take man, the powerful, independent, and invincible controller of his destiny, along comes one lone cancer cell, and our man is no more.

"Michael Zasloff, a biochemist with the National Institute of Health, recently made a fantastic discovery. While working with the African Clawed Frog, he noticed that they never suffered infections. Even when researchers performed surgery on then and returned them to murky, bacteria-filled waters, these frogs remained free from disease. Two months after making his observation, Zasloff discovered that the frog's skin secretes a family of antibodies that protect it from infection. When the frog feels threatened, it emits a white fluid that kills all known forms of bacteria.

"Being a Jewish Boy, and a bit entrepreneurial, he started a pharmaceutical company, and named these antibodies: Magenim, from the Hebrew word Magen. (As in Magen Dovid, shield of David.)

"Isn't that amazing; a frog that can't get an infection? A small, seemingly insignificant creature that is impervious to disease. No matter what bacteria or virus that you expose it to, it will not contract an illness. I want you think about how many people died of infection over the millennia. Before penicillin, it was probably the greatest killer on the face of this planet. Even now, don't we suffer from all different types of infections and illnesses?

"So why not put these same antibodies in man? We see that God is capable of creating an organism that is completely protected from disease—He did it for the little frog. Wouldn't it have been kind to give this to man as well? Wouldn't man's stay on this planet have been improved? Wouldn't he have lived longer, and been able to enjoy life more, without the constant threat of sickness and death looming over his head?

"If you were to tell me, that God wasn't wise enough to figure out all of the answers to man's problems, it would be one thing. But we see a world replete with His wisdom. We see these very wonders in abundance in the natural world, yet man was given some strengths, and not others. Doesn't it make you wonder; why?

"Here is something even more interesting. Scientists are now able to identify and measure the effects that certain chemicals have upon our moods. When I am happy there is actually a chemical change in my brain. There are different ways to cause the release of these chemicals, one is through medication, another is simply through exercise. After a sustained period of physical activity, the brain starts to release these chemicals, and the Thalamus, that part of the brain that relays sensory inputs, reacts bringing about a sensation of mild euphoria. Athletes are well aware of this; they call it runner's high.

"Now, I want to ask you a very simple question: we are told over and over again that God is far more merciful than anyone we could ever imagine. We are told that God loves his creations as a father loves a child. So couldn't God, in his infinite wisdom and kindness, just have given us all a bigger gland that would constantly release this joy activator, and we would be forever happy?

"Why not? It makes no difference to God. He is creating the gland anyway, why not just make it a little bigger, and that would put an end to so much misery in the world.

"Imagine this: you wake up in the morning, stretch out your arms and that gland secretes a nice big dose.

'Wow! How great to be alive!'

"You sit down to a glass of orange juice and another wave of euphoria comes over you.

'Wowwwwwww!!!!'

"Why not? Why not create man that way? It is clear that God has the capacity to do it. With this increased level of chemicals in his brain man would truly be able to live a life of pleasure and comfort. So why not give it to him?

"And while we are asking questions about man, why don't we ask about pain? Did you ever get a headache that wouldn't go away? What do we need that for? In fact why create pain at all? Granted, some pain is important as a warning system; it keeps us from harm, but there are many situations where pain doesn't serve a productive role at all. Have you ever known someone in chronic pain? The type of pain that prevents them from functioning, their whole life focused on ways of alleviating this debilitating anguish that consumes them? What possible benefit is there in that pain? Why create it? And, if it was created, why not make some kind of shut off mechanism? In such a complex and sophisticated system, as the 100 billion cells that make up the central nervous system, I am sure that God could have put in a timer that would stop the transmission of pain after say, five minutes.

"To show you how strong this question is, let's say that I was given the opportunity to design man. Let's imagine that I was given the chance to take all of the wonders that we see in this world and was allowed to put them together to make man. At the risk of sounding irreverent, I think I would do a much better job, than God did. I think that I could put together man in a way that he would be better suited for life in the real world.

"Imagine a booming voice comes from heaven saying:

'RABBI!'

'yes...'

'I HEAR THAT YOU HAVE MANY COMPLAINTS ABOUT THE WAY THAT I DID THINGS.'

'ahhh... No sir, not complaints, I just was wondering out loud...'

'IF YOU THINK THAT YOU CAN DO BETTER—THEN GO AHEAD, YOU MAKE MAN!'

"And so I set out to create man. Using only features that I can find already in this world; I get to pick and choose putting together a new man.

"Wow, what a man I would make! I wouldn't create a puny, weak, little man. My man would be as strong and indestructible as a bear. He would be as fast as a cheetah, and as brave as a lion. I would give him teeth like a shark, an immune system like the African Clawed frog. He would have super sensitive hearing like a bat, and he would be able to go for weeks without water like a camel. He wouldn't have a problem with pain, not my man; I would give him an automatic shut off switch. But more than that he would have a joy gland as large as a coconut. With a constant supply of joy, he would be as happy as a lark all day long. Oh, another thing, laziness? Not in my man. I would give him the energy level of an ant, why he would work all day without tiring—only at night does he stop to rest. Anger? No. I don't think that would do him any good, I would get rid of that part all together. What about competition and jealousy? Not a chance, too many people have been killed over the millennia because of that. Arrogance? No way. He would be humble as pie. What a man he would be!"

David looked at me laughing and said, "You are right that does sound a bit irreverent."

"David, I'm not posing this question for the sake of being disrespectful, but to bring home a key point: it is clear that God is capable of all these features, as he placed them in other species. So why didn't He mix and match them, take the best of each, and then blend them together to form the pinnacle of creation—man? It seems that so much wisdom went into making man exactly as he is. As if God purposefully created man in the state that he is in; strong, yet fragile; independent, yet so dependent; master of the earth, yet contingent upon it for his very survival.

"The key question is what does God have in mind for man? Man, who has the capacity to find joy and also to suffer. Man, who lives with the full gamut of human weakness that entraps generation after generation, so often ending in war and destruction. Man who is this unique conglomeration of strength and weakness, why create him in this fine balance?

"David, I think we are here. I think that we are ready to address that one major question: why did God create man? What did He have in mind when he created man and put him here on this planet? But before I offer you my thoughts, I would like to ask you one question."

Chapter 8: Who Are You?

"Who are you?"

"Who am I?"

"Yes, who are you?"

"I'm not sure I know what you mean?" David responded. "I'm a 32 year old lawyer."

I looked at David and said, "I don't want to sound like a lawyer myself, but my question was, who are you? Not what do you do for a living?"

I explained to him, that this is quite a sore subject with me, This phenomenon of our work being our criteria of self definition. Where, *'What-I-do-for-a-living'* becomes, *'Who-I-am.'* I can't tell you how many times I have heard that routine, where the questioner asks: *'Who are you?'* And the person answers: *'I am a lawyer, a doctor, or an Indian chief.'* I find this is far more then a figure of speech. For many people what they do for a living is the very force that shapes their existence. It is how they approach life, how they look at themselves, and how they position themselves in the world. It goes so far as to become the very definition of who they are.

"David," I said, "do you mind if I share with you one of my pet peeves?"

"Please, go ahead."

"As the years go by, I have officiated at many funerals—far more than I wished to have been at. To me, one of the most troubling parts is when people get up to speak about the deceased. This is the moment to sum up the person, to put forth in a few sentences the full contribution that this person has made to his family, to those he affected, to the world at large. I can't tell you the emotion that I feel when someone gets up to the podium and says *'What a good provider he was.'* As if that is the contribution that this person has made to the world. He made money.

"Now don't get me wrong, one of the roles of a person is to provide for his family's needs. As people we do a lot of things—some significant, and some less so. Earning a living and supporting a family is a serious issue, but is that the sum of the person? Is that what you would use as the defining criteria of man? He was a lawyer, an accountant, a stock broker. Should we put that on his tombstone? I know some people do. Isn't that sad? A lion hunts, a cow grazes, and man works. So, he is an extension of the animal kingdom, just another one of the inhabitants of this planet, trying to feed himself. There's got to be more to life than that. There has to be some higher purpose, some greater meaning than just going to work each day, making money, then spending it, then getting up again, making more money, spending that too—and then we die.

"What makes this even sadder is when you take the height of creation: Man, and reduce him to being a thing, whether it be a job, a profession, or a career, you are so lowering the person by limiting him to one dimension. Is this Man, for whom, the Bible tells us, it was fit to create an entire world? Is this Man, who we are taught, can reach spiritual heights greater than angels? This is a beaver, busy at his dam; a worker bee gathering pollen; an ant bringing in some prize to the nest. You have eliminated all of the 'Greatness of Man.' What about relationships, family, friends? What about kindness? What about making a contribution to others? What happened to helping, to being committed to a cause, to life beyond the work place? How much different is this then enslaving a human? Shackling him to a functional role, like a beast of burden. You exist to work, to do your mundane labor, toil at your task, go through the grind, and then go home to rest up for another day of chores. There's got to be more to life than this.

"So, David, let me repose the question. I know that you are six foot two, weigh 185 pounds, you are handsome, and have brown hair. I certainly recognize that, and I also know that you were born with certain talents and strengths. You are an intelligent, articulate, personable young man. But I want you to stretch, to reach out, beyond today, beyond all that you are currently involved with; past your career, past your getting married and one day raising a family. I want you to reach deep into your inner essence and ask a deep fundamental question: who am I?"

"Rabbi, I'm not sure I know what you mean by who am I? If you mean my spirit, my essence; I guess you could say I am a composite of life experiences and upbringing, a certain level of education, intelligence and personality... I have a way of thinking based on the way I was brought up... I feel passionately about certain issues based on certain values and beliefs... I approach life in a particular way because of my outlook and temperament..."

By the look on David's face I could tell that I only widened the gap between us. "OK," I said, "I want you to try something for me, it may be unpleasant but I think that it will help bring out this point. Let's imagine for a moment, that you are in a car accident, a terrible tragic collision, and you lose both of your legs. You wake up in a hospital room, and now realize that you will spend the rest of your life in a wheel chair. Are you still alive? If your physical condition changes, changes so radically, that everything that you have done up to now has to be rethought, reexamined, and you now have to change your entire life, are you David Goldstein, still alive?"

"Yes, of course, I would be living a different lifestyle but yes, I would still be alive," David answered.

"OK," I continued, "Let's take this one step further. In this horrific accident not only do you lose your legs, but you lose both of your arms as well. Imagine that you are a quadriplegic, are you, still alive?"

"Well, I have to imagine that life would be extremely difficult," David said as he lapsed into thought. After a while he responded, "Yes, I would still be alive."

I looked across to David and said, "I recently read a book, called *The Diving Bell*, written by a French author who had been the editor of a highly respected magazine in Paris. He wrote this book after being in a tragic car accident that left him paralyzed. He describes waking up after being in a coma for three days, only to find that he has no control over his body. He can't move his arms or legs, he can't sit up, he can't even move his head, he is in a state of paralysis. The only part of his body that he has any control over is his left eyelid—he can blink.

"The book is a chronicle of his days in this state, the ups the downs, his daily struggles and travails. He describes that his condition isn't that uncommon, in fact, it has a name: 'Locked-in Syndrome,' because the victim is locked into his or her own body.

"His is one of the first known cases where the patient is left with some ability to communicate to those outside of himself—he could signal with his eye. A speech therapist devised a system where he was able to express his thoughts. She would hold up a card with the alphabet on it. She would move her finger slowly down the card, when she got to a letter that he wanted to express, he would blink, telling her this was the letter he wished to express. In this manner he was able to 'talk', to tell those around him his needs and thoughts.

"It is inspiring that throughout his ordeal, he is able to maintain a sense of humor. He recounts giving each nurse a name, based on the care or gruffness they showed him. Some are angels of mercy; some are mere robots, and one he names: Attila the Hun. He describes the sharp retorts that cross his mind as visitors stand there pitying him. Throughout the book we see his emotional highs and lows. He recounts, enjoying some of the simplest pleasures in life. At one point, he asks to be taken out to the board walk, willingly suffering through twenty minutes of excruciating pain, being jostled in his wheelchair, just to be close enough to the concession stand to be able to smell the heavenly aroma of french fries.

"He tells of the mixed feeling of extreme joy and pain, when his children come to visit. He so intensely enjoys seeing them, to watch them frolic, yet it pains him that he is not able to hold them, and run his fingers through their hair.

"David, was he alive when he was in this state, locked in, shut away from the world, was he, the person still alive?"

David, sat there lost in thought for awhile. By the look on his face, I could see that he understood where I was going with this. "Yes, Rabbi", he responded, "he was alive."

"David," I said, "do you know how alive he was? He was so alive during this period of his life, that he wrote a book. That entire book that became a best seller in France and was later translated into English, was written by a man whose only method of communication was by a blink of an eye. He would compose the sentences and paragraphs in his mind, and then in the afternoon his secretary would stand for hours on end taking dictation—letter by painstaking letter. In this state he felt such intense emotions that he had to share them with the world. Is there any greater tribute to his being alive, than his book?

"David, I want you to imagine for a moment that it is you who are locked in. You can't move your legs, your feet, your hands, and you can't speak—you are totally shut in. Yet, you are still here, you are thinking, feeling, remembering happy times and sad. People come into the room and you are glad that they have come. You wish to say things to them; a different message to each of them. Now David, let's analyze this carefully," I continued. "Your body is useless, your arms and legs lie there limp, you can't move a muscle. So in a sense your body is dead, and yet you are alive. The question is what part of you is alive?"

"Well, Rabbi, I have to admit that I never thought in those terms, I always thought of my life in the sense of being in this body, being a fully functional human being. But, you are right, I would still be alive. As that man wrote an entire book in this condition, I would still be alive, and yet, it seems very hard to relate to myself being alive in that state. I guess you are getting at the idea that my inner spirit would still be alive."

"David, it's even simpler than that, the person that would be alive would be **YOU**. The very same you who is sitting in that chair across from me. The very same you who feels joy or sadness. The same you who thinks, plans, and aspires. When I talk about you, I mean you, who lives inside that body. I don't mean your legs and arms, head and chest, I mean you. We become so accustomed to things as they are that we rarely make this distinction, but the reality is that you are not your body. You are housed in your body. You tell your arms to move. You tell your legs to walk. You tell them to go faster or slower. but, it is you, who controls your body.

"David," I said, "I think we are ready for the answer."

Chapter 9: Purpose of it all

I reached up to the book shelf and pulled down a well worn copy of the *Path of the Just*, an 18th century work by Rabbi Luzzato. I asked David if he had ever heard of this book.

"No, I don't think that I have," David responded.

"Let me introduce this work to you," I said handing it to him. "This is considered by many to be one of the greatest volumes on Jewish belief written in the last 500 years. It is so profound, so deep and far reaching, yet it is written in concise and simple terms, a true masterpiece. In his introduction, the author explains to us that none of the ideas that he presents are his own, rather he has compiled concepts from a wide range of Jewish learning, and placed them together in a readable format. That could be the reason this work, is almost universally accepted as the first and final word in Jewish thought.

"David, I want to read to you the opening few paragraphs." I pulled off my glasses and began reading aloud:

'The source of all religious observance is for it to become clear to a person why God placed him in this world, and what is expected from him.

'What our Sages have taught us is that man was created to take pleasure from God, and find joy in His presence, for that is the true joy, and the greatest pleasure that can be found. The place of that joy is the world to come, as that was specifically created for this function. This is what our sages have taught us, (Avos) "This world is like a corridor to the World To Come."

'The means, that lead man to this goal are the Mitzvahs (commandments) that God has given us. The place for doing these Mitzvahs is only in this world.

'Therefore man was placed in this world first, so that by the mediums that are provided for him here, he will be able to reach the place which has been prepared for him, which is the world to come.'

I paused, took off my glasses, and said, "David, there it is, put out clearly and succinctly. God created man, not for his place in this world, rather for his place in the world to come. To enjoy of the good that he has earned in this world. This world exists for the purpose of allowing man to reach his goal, to grow and perfect himself here, and then enjoy that perfection for eternity. To the extent that I use this world to perfect myself, I will enjoy that state for eternity."

David looked up at me and said, "I now understand why you asked me to imagine myself locked into my body without the ability to move; you were doing that to help me visualize my soul without being limited to my body."

"That's correct," I said, "But I find the word soul to be misleading. When people use that word they tend to think of some other part of them—almost like a distant cousin, or alter ego. As in, *'I had better not do something sinful, because my soul will suffer.' The Path of the Just* is teaching us that, after my body dies, it isn't my soul that will live on after me—"I" will live on. "I" will live on and enjoy the presence of God, in accordance to the amount that I refined myself during my existence in this world. "I". Not my soul, not my body, but 'I."

"I'm not sure I understand what you mean," David said. "What am I but my soul?"

Chapter 10: "I" Am Not My Body

"You are your Soul," I said. "The problem is that it is difficult to properly understand that concept. Let me show you what I mean.

"Imagine that I were to stand up right now and start screaming at you, calling you every nasty name in the book. What would happen?" I asked.

"Assuming that you were serious," David responded, "I would feel pretty badly."

"Exactly, David! Don't you see, you hit the nail on the head. "I" would feel badly. Not your arm, not your leg, not your chest, not your nerves and synapses, not your emotions. "I". "I", may feel through my hands and feet, "I" may taste with my tongue, "I" may smell with my nose, but it is "I", that smells, "I" that feels, "I" that taste. You use your body to bring you these sensations, but it is "I" that experiences them. Who am "I"? I'm not my legs, chest, head, or even my brain; those are tools that "I" use. They are things attached to me that "I" control. They bring me input from the physical world, but they are not me; just like my eyes are tools that I see with, so too, my mind is a tool that I think with. They don't define me. "I", am the master of the ship. "I" am the one who occupies this body and controls my destiny.

"When my body dies, "I" will live on. "I" will enjoy the fruits of my labor on this earth. The point is that it isn't my emotions or my spirit or even my inner soul, it is "I", the part of me that thinks and feels.

"There was a cute novel, written years ago, that illustrates this point. The story line revolves around a young professional football player. One day he is riding his bike around a sharp curve in a tunnel, and he is headed straight into the path of an oncoming car. Assuming that he was going to crash, the Angel of Death takes him, a split second before the actual collision. When they get to heaven, the heavenly court recognizes that an error has been made. Any normal person would have died in that crash, but he, being a professional athlete, has instincts that are so developed, that at the last instant, he would have veered away and would not have gotten hit by the car. He would have lived through that event, therefore he deserves to remain alive.

"Having no other choice, they send him back to this world. Searching for another person close in age, whose time is in fact up, the best that they could come up with is a wealthy, pampered snob living in an exclusive mansion, with an entire staff of butlers and maids. So, they put him back into the body of this rich man.

"The cute part of the story is how he plans to get this flabby, soft body, that he now occupies, into shape for the Super Bowl, which is only three weeks away. So he has these prim and proper servants, running football drills with him on the front lawn of the stately mansion.

"David," I said, "could *you* imagine *yourself* occupying someone else's body; the same essence of *you* being transported into a different being?"

"Well," David responded, "I never thought in those terms, but I could see myself being in someone else's body, occupying a different life."

"You see, David, that is the point, *you* do occupy a body. It happens to be the one that *you* were born into. But again, it is *you* that lives in *your* body. You are distinct and separate from *your* arms, legs, and chest, and that is because *you* are not physical, *you* are spiritual.

"We are so used to mixing up "I", with our body, that it becomes hard to separate them; we have trouble remembering that, in fact, they are separate entities. For that reason, from a scientific perspective, it is difficult to define death. Is it when the heart stops beating? Is it when the brain waves stop? What about a person whose is kept on a respirator, in a state of coma for ten *years*, are they dead or alive?

"Picture this case: A twenty year old woman is in a coma, yet all of her organs are functioning: A respirator is keeping her breathing, various drugs are keeping her heart beating, and all of her body parts are now doing what they should be doing. From a medical point of view, there is no reason why this person shouldn't be breathing, yet she isn't. The body lying there seems to be alive. But is it? Physiologically it is. There is a pulse, there is blood pressure, all of the bodily functions are working. Yet she is dead, but is she?

"I find it ironic, when a ninety two year old woman dies peacefully in her sleep and there is no known medical reason, yet the Death certificate demands: CAUSE OF DEATH. What do you write? Congestive heart failure? Respiratory arrest? In a sense that is what happened, but if you really want to define death, it is the spirit, she, her essence no longer occupies her body. From a purely medical point of view, the cause of death is UNKNOWN. When two cars collide at sixty miles an hour the cause of death is obvious. The body that houses the spirit is so broken that it can no longer hold on. But, what happens when a five year old, perfectly healthy child, suddenly dies, for no apparent reason? What happens when a teenager lies down to sleep, and doesn't wake up? We don't have a cause of death. There is no reason why the body shouldn't be humming along as healthy as a song bird. Yet the sprit is gone, the "I" is no longer there.

"From a scientific perspective, it is difficult for us to define death, because we are applying physical measurements to something that exists in a different dimension. It is like trying to weigh light. It would be foolish to calculate how many pounds a strong beam of light weighs. You could measure luminosity, but weight is the wrong criteria to measure the strength of light. So too, you can't use physical instruments to measure the "I". You can't add blue dye to the beaker, heat it, and see what the reaction will be. You can use a gauge to measure blood pressure. You can run tests on gas levels in the blood. You can measure breathing efficiency. But what test do you run to see if "I", the essence of the person, is still there? How do you measure whether that part of the person, the inner part, is still there? That part is not physical, so none of the tests or guides can tell us anything about it. "I" is from a different dimension, so any attempt to measure "I" through physical criteria is bound to fail.

"The key point to realize is that "I" is not physical. We get so accustomed to thinking of ourselves as physical beings that we actually think that "I" is physical. "I" is not, "I" is spiritual. The point that the *Path of the Just* is making to us, is that when my body dies, "I", will live on forever. Just like weight is not relevant to light, so too, death is not relevant to the spirit of man.

"One of the classic works on Judaism, written by Rabbi Israel Salanter, describes death as being similar to 'taking off a coat.' The same "I" that is housed within my body will emerge and in that state, live on. The same "I" that now experiences feelings of joy, pain, sorrow, or happiness, will live, step out of this body, and continue to experience the full pallet of human emotions. "I" will experience them. Not my alter ego, not my distant cousin, "I". The same "I" that is speaking to you right now.

"The sole reason "I" was put on this planet was to grow. "I" was placed in this body, given this one chance to perfect myself here, and in that state, live on forever. Whatever level of perfection I have attained, I will enjoy for eternity. "I" will be deeply pained by my shortcomings, and "I" will be immensely proud of my achievements. This alone is the reason why God created us and put us in this world.

"David, if we fully appreciated the significance of this one point, it would change our entire view point on life, and would affect every decision we make. It would impact our values and beliefs. It would significantly change what we strive for, and what we consider important. In short, it would have a deep and profound effect on every aspect of our life.

Chapter II: Pleasure Without a Body

I was out of town the following week, so we didn't get back together until two weeks later. When David came in, and looked ready to go, it brought me back to when he was a high school student.

"Rabbi," David said, "when we first started meeting, I didn't anticipate our discussions going quite this way. I kind of assumed that we would be talking about rituals and traditions... While I am fascinated by all of this; I never thought that it had much to do with Judaism. In any case, I am starting to get a grip on these ideas, but there is one point that is bothering me:

"I have no trouble dealing with "I" as being separate from my body. I can even see myself existing apart from my body. I guess I can relate to the concept of "I" living on, after my body dies. The one area that I get stuck on, is that line that we read in our last session: 'that man was created to take pleasure from God, and find joy in His presence, for that is the true joy and the greatest pleasure that can be found.' I find it difficult to grasp this concept of *enjoying* anything after my body dies. When I think of enjoying something, I keep getting stuck in a physical mode. I think of sitting down to eating a steak and enjoying it, but if I no longer occupy my body, it seems hard to imagine enjoying anything."

"David," I said, "The reason it is difficult is because we get so accustomed to life as it is, that it is hard for us to imagine it any other way. And so it takes a while to relate to enjoying life in a very different modality. Let me try to explain it to you with a metaphor:

"Imagine for a moment that you are in court. It is the biggest case in your life. In fact, the issues being debated are so pivotal to the practice of law, that the court proceedings are being video taped. Yesterday, the judge asked you for a brief, outlining the key position in your case. The judge now resumes court and you are standing there when he says in a solemn voice:

'Mr. Goldstein, I have been a judge now for ten years, and have practiced law for twenty years before that.' (Your heart is now racing, you have no idea where this is going.) 'In all my years on the bench,' the judge continues, 'I have never read such a well organized, lucid, and logically compelling brief, as the one that you have presented. Mr. Goldstein you are to be congratulated.' At that moment, the judge and all of the onlookers in the courtroom burst into applause.

"David, at that point what do you think you would feel?"

"I would imagine I'd be one happy guy," David chuckled.

"I'm sure you would be," I agreed. "Likely you would be feeling an intense sense of joy, a feeling that begins somewhere deep within you and starts to spread; an elation so deep and so profound that it transcends time and place. You wouldn't walk out of the courtroom that day, you would float out.

"What part of you experienced that? Was it your hands? Your feet? Your head? Was it your chest, or arms? It wasn't any part of your body that felt it. It was you. You felt pleasure. You were ecstatic. This is an example of an "I" pleasure; a completely non physical pleasure that "I" experience. It is a pleasure that has no connection to your physical state of being, and so, it is not dependent upon your body. The essence of you experience it, and that part, the "I", lives on forever and enjoys the work you put in, while in this world.

"If you think about it, there are many pleasures that "I" experiences. Listening to music can be a very moving one. Have you ever come home after a long day at work, kicked off your shoes, cranked up the stereo, and just gotten lost in the music? You may have started off in a lousy mood. You turned on a favorite album and soon, your foot began moving with the beat. Before you knew it you were humming along.

"Then you started to move with the music, by now you were in a different mood. You were floating, up there, flowing with the music.

"That was you enjoying an experience that clearly is not physical. Not your body, but you. "I" was experiencing pleasure. There are many things that "I" feel that are not physical in nature. The full gamut of emotions, from love—to hate—to rage, and jealousy, these are things that "I" feel. "I" feel proud of my accomplishments. "I" feel appreciative of kind gestures from others, and "I" feel hurt by words that people say. It isn't my heart that feels the pain. We may euphemistically use expressions like a broken heart, but what we really mean is that "I" have been hurt. Me.

"Can you remember a time when you were deeply embarrassed? You said something that was totally inappropriate, and by the time the words came off your lips, you could already feel a burning sensation spreading. It started in your forehead then spread down your face. You sensed something hot emanating from within you trying to burn out. As it spread, it seared, and you felt an intense pain.

"David, it wasn't your heart that was feeling it, it wasn't your chest, it wasn't even your soul. It was **You.** The feeling was so real, that your entire being was enveloped in it; you wished there was a hole you could climb into and never come out of. The point is that feelings are not dependent on your body. Even if you didn't have legs you would feel the pain; even if your hands were numb you would still cringe. You would still feel that same horrible, sinking feeling; because **You** are feeling it. "I" am experiencing something that is not physical in nature or tied to this world in which we live. These sensations, many enjoyable, and some quite painful, are all examples of "I" feeling things that are not physical.

"That sense of elation you experience when you find out you won the Lotto; the emotion you feel when you meet your daughter for the first time in the delivery room; that utter sense of joy and fulfillment, the complete feeling of jubilation—can we even describe such experiences? The heart feels them, or more accurately "I" feel them; but they are not physical. They are inner conditions that are so fine they almost defy definition, but they sure are real, and "I" feel them.

"When I am separated from my body, I will live on and feel all of those same emotions. I will rejoice in my accomplishments, or suffer for my shortcomings, but it is "I", that will feel pain, and "I" that will feel pleasure, just as I enjoy these sensations on this earth.

"When we talked about the French editor, being locked in his body, didn't he experience the full spectrum of human emotions? If we could have been there with him and felt his emotional state when he was informed that his book had been published—that his message had been heard, and his plight was now being shared by millions. Could we describe that deep sense of satisfaction?

"It is that same sense of deep, profound joy that I will feel, if I use my life appropriately here.

"If you think about it, any joy that we experience is not physical. Our body feels pleasure, our soul feels joy. Happiness, satisfaction, and serenity; conditions that we value above everything else in life, have little to do with the body. They do not come to us through our body, and they are not dependent upon our physical state. Most of what makes us human, those feelings and sensations that separate us from the animal kingdom, are not physical in nature, and do not depend upon our body for their existence.

"So when you ask what it means that "I" will enjoy the work I have done when I leave my body. We are talking about "I". "I" will feel joy and pleasure; the same part of me that experiences these emotions in my current state, Me. And the emotions that I will feel are more intense than anything I can feel while I am locked into my body here—here I am enveloped in a heavy cloak of physicality that does not allow me to feel the full depths of emotions. When I leave this earth and I am stripped of that outer cloak, I will intensely feel all of those emotions.

"We are here in this physical state we occupy for a short time. Inside my body, in my temporary existence, I live. I have the opportunity to grow and accomplish, to perfect the "I" and then forever enjoy that state of perfection that I have reached. I have a few short years here, a chance to make the right choices, grow and perfect myself, and in that state live on for eternity. God custom designed this world with all of the necessary components to allow us to grow. He created all of the opportunities and challenges needed to allow us to perfect ourselves, so that we can enjoy our exalted state when we leave this earth. Much more then a side benefit, or tangential result—this is the purpose of creation. This is why God created this world and put man in it. This is why we are here."

David stopped me and said, "Rabbi, the problem is, this seems so far away. In theory, I can relate to the idea of enjoying something in a non physical existence, I can even accept that God would create us to allow us to perfect ourselves in this world, and then enjoy that state of perfection in the world to come. The problem is that we are talking about a basis of morality, as you have said, something that will affect my life on a day to day basis. These concepts seem too far removed from the world that I live in to change the way that I act or the way that I view life."

Chapter 12: Hello, This is My Funeral

"That is true, David," I responded. "For these concepts to have any effect on my life they must become real—I have to feel them, and that takes a lot of work. By nature we live in the here and now. We tend to feel that the current state of affairs will last forever, and so these types of thoughts seem very far away. To help brings these ideas closer; I want you to try an exercise: Let's imagine a large, carpeted room, with dark drapes on the wall. The lights are muted, the mood is somber. In the front of the room are two candles burning. Gathered are two hundred of your closest friends and relatives, all seated, all listening attentively. All eyes are focused on the front of the room. And there you are, right there in front of everyone—lying in a box. Dead as a door nail. It is your funeral.

"You look around the room, you see your aunts, whom you haven't seen in years. There is your best friend Bob. You want to run over and hug him, but you can't. You can't move; you can't speak. More than anything, you are scared, terrified is a better word. Somewhere in the back of your mind, you always knew this moment would come; but not so soon. Not now. I'm not ready, not yet.

"There are people gathered that you haven't seen in years, they're all here. Your brother Jonathan, who you haven't spoken to in five years, is sitting in the front row. You want to hug him and tell him that you are so sorry for all of those harsh words that you spoke to each other over the years. There is your cousin Marni, whom you grew up with. She looks dreadful and is sobbing uncontrollably. You want to comfort her and tell her it is not so bad. *'Come on, Marni, it happens to all of us.'*

"You wonder, is this real? Am I here? Is this really happening? I can think, I can see everyone. I know they are here. I can even hear them. I am conscious. Wait, I must be alive, I can think, and hear, I know these people are all here. So how can I be dead? You hear the speakers say all of those nice things about you, memories of you when you were younger, good things that you did in your lifetime, and you want to scream out, *'Stop! This can't be happening. Stop!'*

"In this one electrifying moment you come to the realization that life has an end. You understand that you were here, on this planet for a few short years. You had a mission, and a goal, with a particular function to accomplish, and now it is over.

"You watch as they carry you out. All of your friends gather around the coffin, each one putting a shoulder under it. You hear them say those words, *'He was so young.' 'I can't believe it.' 'What a tragedy.'* You watch as the crowd moves out of the funeral home. You see them, their faces ashen, holding on to the casket—your casket. They put you in the back of a hearse. The crowd gets into their cars and follows you to the cemetery.

"They all gather around an open grave. They lay your casket out. You watch as they gather on each side, grabbing the cloth bands that are holding up your coffin. Slowly, they start to lower you into the ground. Then it hits you. At that moment the truth comes crashing through. It is over, my life, all that I have known it to be—all that I have come to expect—life itself is over. My life. My life is over! It wasn't supposed to end, not really, certainly not like this.

"Now the real panic begins. *'Stop!'* You want to scream. *'Stop! What are you doing? This isn't real. Stop it. I am alive! What are you doing? Don't put me in there. I won't be able to get out! Stop. How am I going to breathe in there? Stop! Stop! Stop!'* They don't stop. They continue to lower the casket deeper. You can no longer see their faces. *'Stop. Help! Someone, please make them stop!'* Your mind races a thousand thoughts, this can't possibly be real. Life. Life itself. What is happening? This can't be. You feel a jolt as the casket hits bottom.

"Someone picks up a shovel, turns the spade part backwards, and begins dropping dirt. *'What are you doing?'* you want to scream. You hear the first drops of dirt on the casket. *'Stop!'* Then another. The sound is deafening. This wasn't supposed to happen. Not to me. Not yet! More dirt, as the sound fades. Isn't anyone going to make them stop?! Again and again, the dirt drops down. It starts to form a layer, until the casket is completely covered.

"Then it happens. That one moment you lived your life running from. That one moment, that in the back of your mind, somewhere, somewhere deep inside you always knew would come. It now happens. You separate. You leave your body behind in the dirt. You, the "I" that thinks and feels departs from your body. You feel a new wave of terror sweep over you as you think, what comes next?"

I stopped for a long time. While I knew this wasn't a comforting thought to David or to anyone for that matter, I also knew how important, how pivotal this exercise is, in truly living one's life to its potential, but I really didn't want to go any further.

I said, "David, why don't we stop here."

Chapter 13: WYSIWYG - What You See Is What You Get

Well we all have a face
That we hide away forever
And we take them out and show ourselves
When everyone is gone.

—Billy Joel, *Faces of the Stranger*

"David, isn't it interesting that we have different faces that we show to people? I have found the same person to be very different around me as when they are in other company. A man might be as sweet as sugar regarding his dealings with the Synagogue. Then later I find out from his employees that he is a terror to work for. Or, how many times have we seen a neighbor who we knew for years, and only after their divorce do we find out they were physically abusive to their spouse?

"We spend much effort on hiding our true selves from other people, and if we are skilled, we can get away with it for a good while. The reason for this is that you can't see who I really am. You can see my face, my exterior, but what is really going on inside me is hidden from you. I may be thinking all kinds of thoughts in my mind, but my face, my outside, presents a very different picture. What would it be like if you could see me—see me for exactly what I was—with all of my good qualities and my bad as well? What if you could see past that smile affixed to my face, and see what I was really thinking in my heart? What if you could see me when I was doing a 'good act', and you were shocked to see that the real motivating force was not a desire to help people, but a drive for honor?

"Did you ever hear the expression: 'People usually have two reasons for doing something—one that sounds good, and then the real reason.' I don't mean to put anyone down, however, the reality is that many motives are mixed into our actions. Rarely does it cause me embarrassment, because I can hide my true motives from you. But what if for a moment you could see right into the core of who I am, and you saw it all? Could you imagine the embarrassment that even the most refined person would feel?

"To me personally, one of the most frightening thoughts in life is that when I leave this earth, I will be standing exposed, naked for all to see. The "I" that we talked about, me, will live on long after my body dies, and I will be there exactly as I am here, but without anything to hide behind. You, and everyone else, will see me exactly for who I am. Here, I wear this thick coat of a human body, and it covers me up so you can't see me, but when this coat is peeled away and "I" emerge, you will see me stripped naked of my learned behaviors, unable to hide behind any facades. Who I am, and what I am, will be clear for all to see. I will be as beautiful as I have made myself, or as ugly as I have shaped myself into being.

"The reason we were put on this earth is to mold the "I". That is the sole reason that God created this world; to give us the ability to change, to fashion ourselves. We don't realize the effect that our actions have upon us, but every situation in life that causes us to make a choice, is part of the molding process. We are constantly being formed. The **decisions** that I make, the **words** that I say, and the **actions** that I take, all have their effect on me. They shape me, mold me, and create me into who I am now, and who I will be for eternity.

"Unfortunately, many of us take the attitude: *'This is who I am, this is my temperament... you can't change a leopard's spots.'* We fail to recognize how much *'who I am'* is in my control, and how great the impact of living life as I do, has on my essence. How many times have we heard the line: *'I wish I wouldn't lose my temper, but what can I do that's my nature.'* Now, to a certain degree that is true. Each person is born with a different nature. If we were to list all of the personality traits: Kindness, Cruelty, Generosity, Compassion, Humility, Arrogance, Anger, and Jealousy... and then we were to create a ranking system of one to one hundred, with one hundred being perfection. We would find that each person has natural inclinations in each of these areas. By natural temperament, Sally might rank a fifty in Anger, a thirty in Kindness, a forty in Jealousy, and a twenty five in Humility. That is her starting point; her ground zero. What happens during her lifetime is that she will be shaped when she is younger, and as she gets older she takes over the shaping process, so that she is molding herself throughout her life. By the time she is a mature woman her rating would be very different then it was when she started at birth. Now she might have improved her Anger to twenty, in terms of Humility an eighty, in terms of Generosity a ninety, or perhaps the opposite.

"In each one of these areas we are extremely malleable. The very essence of each trait is subject to change. A person can go from being selfish and cruel, to being giving and caring. A person might have started life with a fierce temper, and during their lifetime have made great strides, until the flames of anger have been cooled down. Now they stand in front of you, a much improved person. A man may have started out with a tendency towards Arrogance, and by using his life appropriately he may well have reached the heights of Humility.

See Diagram 1 on Page 80

"We were put on this planet to grow. We were put here to shape our very essence and to mold ourselves, and in that state, live on.

"Every action affects my very personality. When I get angry, there are two results that come about: one is that I raise my voice and say words that are damaging, words that hurt another person. That alone is very grave. Then there is a second effect: I have made a change in myself. I have made a change in my temperament, in my essence. Sometimes the change is slight, sometimes greater, but in either case I have been affected, and my anger, will now be stronger within me. The next time a similar situation arises it will be easier for me to get angry, and my anger may be deeper and longer lasting.

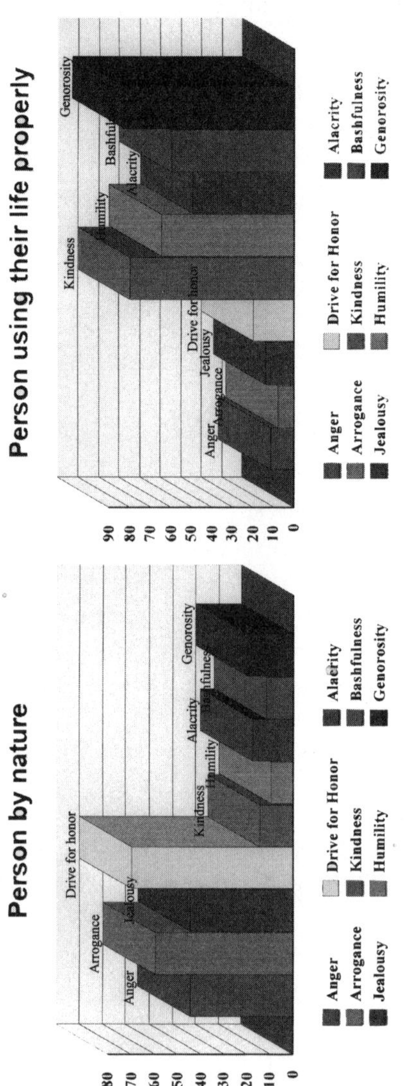

Person using their life properly
0
10
20
30
40
50
60
70
80
90
Anger
Arrogance
Jealousy
Drive for honor
Kindness
Humility
Alacrity
Bashful
Generosity
Anger
Arrogance
Jealousy
Drive for Honor
Kindness
Humility
Alacrity
Bashfulness
Genorosity
Person by nature
0
10
20
30
40
50
60
70
80
Anger
Arrogance
Jealousy
Drive for honor
Kindness
Humility
Alacrity
Bashfulness
Genorosity
Anger
Arrogance
Jealousy
Drive for Honor
Kindness
Humility
Alacrity
Bashfulness
Genorosity

"This is true for each of the character traits. They are almost like muscles; the more you use them the stronger they become. If a woman acts in a kindly manner, again there are two results. One is she did a good act, which in itself has great merit and importance. Secondly, she brought about a change in her inner essence. She is now a kinder person. The "I" has changed. If a man acts in a boastful manner, going into the routine of, *'Do you know who I am... Do you know how big, how important, and how significant I am?'* The net result isn't only the ugly face of Arrogance, additionally, each time he gets into one of his bragging modes, it is shaping his essence. He is fashioning his ego, making it larger, so that he becomes haughtier. And he is a changed person. Not the outside, not the face, arms, or hands but the essence of him is now changed.

"When it comes to physical changes we are very much attuned to this process. I know that if I go to the gym and follow a prescribed exercise program, my physique will change. If I lift weights my biceps will increase in size, my chest will become more muscular, my waist will become thinner. The change won't be noticeable the first time that I come home from the gym, but each workout causes a very slight increase in muscle tissue and decrease in body fat.

"In regards to the human personality it works the same way, every action affects me. Each decision that I make changes me, shapes me, and molds me. In some areas, thought can have an even greater effect than actions. With Arrogance in particular, more of the damage comes from the thought process than from actions. In our society it is rare that a person can assume a role of 'lording it over someone else,' so the outward manifestations of conceit are not as common as in earlier generations, but internally there is plenty of room for this process to go on. When a person thinks to themselves: *'There are few people who are quite as intelligent as I'. 'I outdid even myself this time.' Or, 'I am gorgeous, simply gorgeous.'* These thoughts themselves cause the very nature of the person to change, to become more arrogant.

"However, an important distinction between the example of exercise and personality shaping, is that a person spends only a few hours a day in the gym. Even if my goal is to be in fantastic shape, I might work out five times a week, for a few hours at a time. When it comes to shaping me—molding my personality—this is something that I am doing from the moment I get up in the morning, until the moment I go to sleep at night. Every situation, every interaction with others, every time that I am in a life situation that allows me to choose, my choice has its effect upon me. I am thinking, I am speaking, and I am acting, all of which mold me, shape me, make me into who I am.

"The difficult part is that we are shaping our inner self all day long. If we were to count our interactions with others each day, the number would be in the hundreds. From the moment I get up in the morning until I go back to bed in the evening, I interact with so many different people on many different levels, that it is impossible to keep track. In each one of those situations, my thoughts, words and actions will affect me.

"When we leave this world we are what we made ourselves into. For eternity I will be what I have shaped myself into. You and everyone else will see me exactly for who I am.

"I don't know if you remember the old style word processing programs. To change a font or indent a line you would type in a command next to the word. On the screen the command **{bold}** would appear next to the text, but the printer would recognize the symbol and change the character to bold print. The newer programs came out with a feature called WYSIWYG, or What You See Is What You Get. Now everything was different, if you made a change it appeared on the screen as it would print. Your bold letters were bold, your indented lines were indented, right there as they would print out and WYSIWYG—What You See is What You Get.

"David, that is what happens when we leave this earth—WYSIWYG. What I am, what I made myself into, is what you will see. I spent a life time thinking thoughts, saying words, and doing things; each one leaves its imprint on me. "I" am now very different than I was ten years ago and even more so than I was ten years before that. I have changed. When "I" am stripped of this physical covering then you will be able to see me as I am. "I" will be exactly what I made myself into.

"Think about how much effort we spend on our outward appearances. How many times a day do we look in the mirror, or straighten our tie? It is so important to us. If a man has a bald spot that he covers, and he gets caught in a rain storm, think of the embarrassment he suffers when he walks into the office—hair dripping wet. There are women who won't be caught outside on a bad hair day. Even a stain on our tie or dress causes us much distress, because we look sloppy. We look disheveled, and we are embarrassed. We take pride, and rightfully so, in the way we look.

"All of those things are outside of me. They are external. But, what about something that is me? What about something that is so a part of me that it is my very essence? And, what if it is ugly? What if all can see it and it is black? As I sit here now, you don't see my selfish streak. What about my temper? What about my laziness? It's covered up. You know me here based on my actions. Based on your relationship with me, you take a composite shot of all of my actions and words, and create an image in your mind of who I am. Sometimes you are close, sometimes your are far off, but even if you know a person very well, you can never get it quite right, because you are just guessing at what is going on inside another person.

"But, what if you could see the real me? What if you could watch my mind as I think? What if you could look into the essence of me as I walk in the room, and I go through all of those thoughts that my mind spins out. I think that you would have a very different picture of me. You would see who I truly am. Here I can hide from you. I can shield myself behind the learnt social norms that we are schooled in from our youth. As we mature in life we become very skilled at masking our inner self. Boys are taught at a very young age not to cry. Certainly not in public, and better not at all. Does it mean that they are dead inside? Does it mean that they don't feel things? They still have emotions, but they are socialized to hide what they feel. And we become quite good at hiding who we are from those around us—and often even from ourselves.

"In the world to come there is no hiding, no cover-up—just Truth. You will be able to see me clearly. Not my physical self, that part will be buried in the ground, but me, who I really am, exactly as I am, without makeup, without any touch ups, for the good or for the bad standing there disrobed, bare, exposed for all to see.

"Don't you see, David? We all have things that we don't want the world to see. We all have faces of the strangers that we are embarrassed to show. The frightening part is that if we don't work on ourselves now, if we don't use this life that we were given, for its intended purpose, we will suffer through many moments of embarrassment for eternity, when it is too late to do anything about it, when it is too late to change."

Chapter 14: Actors on the Stage

"Rabbi," David said. "A lot of what you have said about our purpose in this world makes sense. I find the concept of life itself as an opportunity for growth, motivating and inspiring; it gives such meaning to even the mundane things that we do. Just the thought that every interaction with another person leaves an imprint on me, and will show itself in my essence for eternity, is a very powerful catalyst for change. The question that keeps bothering me though is that the system itself seems unfair."

"What do you mean?" I asked.

"Well," David continued, "on a personal level I can't complain, because I feel that I was given a very good lot in life. But, if I look around I see people who aren't as fortunate as I am. I see people born into poverty, who don't have the opportunities that I was given. I see people born with infirmities and handicaps. There are children who are neglected and abused. How can they possibly be expected to perform on the same level, as an individual, born into a comfortable home, with loving nurturing parents? If in fact, God is fully in charge, and put us on this planet to grow, there sure does seem to be a lot of inequality in the world. How do you explain why one person is born with tremendous innate talent, and the capacity to translate it into great accomplishments, while another is so average? It just doesn't seem that we were all given the same chance to grow."

"David," I said, "your question is based on assuming that we are ultimately judged by what we have accomplished in this world, as if there were a standard of measure against which man is judged, but that isn't why we are here. While it is true that God put us on this planet to grow and accomplish, the measure of man isn't how much he accomplished as compared to others. There is only one criterion against which man is measured; how much he grew, in relation to his potential.

"God has custom designed a set of circumstances for each individual, to give him the ultimate setting for his growth and personal perfection. What we are judged by isn't objectively how much we have accomplished—but rather what we accomplished as measured by what we were created to do. How close we came to fulfilling our mission in this life.

"To give you a parable, picture this: Jack Nicholson receives a call from his agent.

'Listen Jack, we just got a great offer. Tons of money, an all cash deal, you get the star role, playing next to the greatest co-stars in the industry. The best part of it is the plot. It's great! The story line really clicks. It's a guaranteed Oscar. I'm sending the script over this morning. Tell me what you think.'

After reading the script, Jack calls his agent back.

'Listen Bob, forget it, no deal.'

'What do you mean?'

'I mean there's no way, no deal. I won't do it.'

'Jack, what is it? Is it the script?'

'No, the script is fine?'

'Is it the other actors?'

'No, they're fine too.'

'So Jack, what is it?'

'What is it? Bob, don't you get it? The guy that you want me to play is penniless and not too bright either. More than that, he's a jerk! I can't stand anyone seeing me that way.'

'But Jack, that's only the part you are playing, it's not you.'

'Bob, forget it, doing this movie means everyone, I mean millions of people are going to see me as a pauper, a creep, and a down and out. I wouldn't be able to stand the embarrassment. Don't even ask me again, I'm not doing it.' Then he hangs up.

"Obviously, this conversation never took place. Because, any actor, as well as any person going to the theater, understands that those people up there on the screen are playing their parts. They aren't judged by how wealthy or poor they are in the movie. They aren't judged by whether their role portrays a life of success or failure. There is one criterion for judging an actor: how well did he play his part. If his role is to play the part of a Savant Idiot, and he does it convincingly, he will win an Oscar for his performance. If his role is to be the most successful man in the world and he isn't real, the critics will rip him to pieces. He is there for only one purpose—to play his role well. He is given a certain backdrop, and a certain set of circumstances—the character has this type of personality, is from this type of background, has this level of intelligence—now go out there and play the part.

"That's what life is about. Each of us was given a specific set of circumstances, and a particular set of criteria. The backdrop is set and we are given the task of playing the role. Born in a particular time period, to a particular family, given a very exact set of parameters—you will be this tall, this intelligent, have this much talent, and so on. Now, go out there and do it! Live you life, ford those streams, cross those rivers, and sail those seas! Live up to your potential. In the end, we are measured by how close we came to accomplishing all that we were capable of.

"Only a fool really believes that he is more intelligent than the next person because of anything that he did. Granted I may have learnt more,

I may have developed my innate intellect to a higher degree than another person. I may have taken the natural talents that God gave me and did more with them than someone else. But, at the end of the day the basics were given to me. An athlete may develop his skills and hone his God given talent—but as Mark McGuire said, after hitting his record shattering seventieth home run: *'The Man upstairs gave Mark McGuire his eye hand coordination.'*

"What I am given credit for is how far I went with what was given to me; how much did I do with the talent that God gave me. Whether I am smarter, richer, or more talented then the next person is irrelevant, the only issue is: How much did I accomplish compared to—**me**, compared to what I was capable of accomplishing, had I used my life appropriately.

"One of the great teachers of 17th century Judaism, the Vilna Gaon, tells us that the most painful moment in a persons life is after they leave this earth; when the heavenly tribunal holds up a picture for them to look at; a picture of a truly exceptional individual. A person of sterling character traits, who shows intelligence, kindliness, and humility—a person of true greatness; a person who brought outstanding goodness to the world and changed the very world in which they lived. Then they say to me, why didn't you do what he did?

"Me?! Little me? What do you want from me? Was I some kind of genius? Was I some kind of powerful leader of men? How could I have done those types of things?

"They answer, one telling and most troubling line: that picture is you. Not you, as you stand here now. Not you as you have lived your life. But, that is you had you become what you were destined to be. That is you, had you accomplished what you were put on this earth for. That is you, had you followed the path for which you were born.

"That moment is the most painful in a person's life, because at that moment, the truth comes crashing through—They understand what they were capable of accomplishing. They can clearly see the purpose of life and recognize what they could have achieved in their stay on this planet. At that one flash point of recognition they truly understand the greatness of man, what he is capable of doing, but then it is too late, life is over."

I let David take this in for a while. My mind was drawn away by the delightful sound of children playing in the Synagogue playground. I was pulled back by David's question.

"How do I put this... I can understand what you are saying about being here to play our role and being judged by those criteria. That answers part of the question, but what about a person born into a poor home, where he doesn't have the opportunity of going to the finest schools? What about a young woman born into a broken home, where there is no proper role model, where life is cheap and meaningless? Is she expected to reach her potential? If, in fact, we are saying that God places every human being on this planet for the purpose of allowing them the opportunity to grow, it sure does seem that there is inequity in the settings that He has provided."

"You are raising a good point, David," I responded. "To understand this, we have to take a step away from life as we know it, and try to understand some of the inner workings of the human personality.

"I want you to imagine for a moment that you, instead of being born to your parents, the Goldsteins, living in this part of history, were born to a different family named the Capones, living in the 1930's in Chicago. Let's imagine even further, that your proud parents named you Alphonse. So, there you were, Al Capone, living in the wild side of Chicago, growing up without any positive influences in your life. Everyone you ever knew was bootlegging, hanging out in bars, or taking bets as a bookie. Certainly your nature, your very temperament was that of an opportunist, and maybe even a little cruel. All that you experienced from the cradle was: *'It's a dog eat dog world out there. You either kill, or get killed.'*

"David, how do you think that you would have turned out?"

David sat back for a moment, and then said, "Well Rabbi, I have to say, I think that I would have turned out pretty much like that infamous gangster, whose name I was carrying."

"I don't think that is true," I responded. "Even if you were given his exact temperament by birth, I wouldn't assume that you would turn out as he did. There were many people who were born into worse situations than Al Capone was, and they didn't turn to a life of crime. In fact, Al Capone was only one of many children, and one of an entire generation of children who grew up in similar circumstances. The vast majority of them blossomed into fine, upstanding, law abiding citizens.

"Al Capone made himself into who he was. It was the process of thousands of small decisions that occurred over the course of a lifetime, but he shaped the person that he became.

"You see, David, we make hundreds of choices each day that we live. By the time we are adults most of our choices are habitual, we no longer consciously choose them. We have long ago created patterns of thought and behavior that shape much of what we do. But, it was us long ago who set up those patterns. It was **us** who made those choices and thereby created the personality that you see in front of you right now. Once we have set up those patterns they are difficult to break, but we did it.

"It all starts with choices that we make. Those choices shape our **thoughts**, our **actions**, and our **habits**, which then shape our very **destiny**, but it all begins with a choice.

"This is what the concept of Free Will really means. Free to choose how we will act. Free to choose who we will become, and thereby free to shape our destiny.

"Do you remember we spoke about a person having an inner sense of right and wrong? Every human, who has ever lived under the sun, instinctively knows what is right and what is wrong. That is the nature of the human. It may be true that Al Capone had a stronger inclination to do things that we consider antisocial. It may even be true that his upbringing made it easier for him to fall into the trap of becoming the sociopath that he was, but it was his choice to make, whether to listen to that Voice Inside, or give in to his natural tendencies.

"Al Capone wasn't born Al Capone, he shaped himself into that personality. Adolph Hitler wasn't born evil. Through a long series of life choices he shaped his thoughts, which shaped his philosophy of life. But, it all starts with choices, and choices on a very small level.

"Let me give you an example from a different perspective. Look out that window," I said, motioning to the long bank of windows on the side of my study.

David looked out to the Synagogue playground.

"What do you see?" I asked.

"I see little children playing."

"Are they angry?"

"No."

"Do they look displeased with themselves or with life in general?"

"No," David answered, "they look quite happy."

"I think that is true. Children on the whole are happy. Not to say they don't have their moments, but a healthy child brought up in a good home, is happy. One of my fondest memories is of my children as toddlers when they would wake up in the morning. While the rest of the house was still asleep, from their crib they would start their melodies—such sweet, happy sounds. Sometimes they would sing snatches of songs, sometimes they would carry on entire conversations with their dolls, or with the world at large. I don't think that I could ever capture such carefree happiness again. Children have such optimism and enthusiasm for life, they so enjoy just being alive.

"Look at the same child ten years later: you are likely to see a different picture. Gone is much of the vibrancy, gone is much of the zest, much of the love of life is out of them. They don't seem to smile quite as often, and they don't laugh as much. I once read a study that on average a child laughs 114 times a day! By the time they are adults the number is a fraction of that. What happened?

"What happened is that they have changed. They are now different. A child is plastic, not only does a child's mind grow in intelligence and perception, their very nature is being molded as they go through their day. Their very personality is being shaped. How they respond, how they react, how they view life, is taking form. Childhood is a shaping, developing process. Not only in the sense of behavior and attitudes, but the very nature, the inner soul of the child is taking shape.

"I am not a big fan of Sigmund Freud, but some of his opinions are telling. A woman came to him with her five year old son and said, *'Doctor, when is the right time to begin his education?'* As the story goes, he responded, *'Madam, you are asking that question five years too late, much of the work has been already done.'*

"David, I want you to understand this as an ongoing process throughout life. Children don't have the intelligence or self control to consciously shape their nature; but as adults we do. Whether we are aware of it or not, we are constantly molding our very personalities. Not only in the areas of happiness, or enthusiasm for life, but across the full gamut of the human condition. Our arms and legs are formed by the time we are adults, but our inner core is constantly subject to growth.

"To show you how far this goes: the Rabbis tells us, that one of the Monarchs in the ancient world heard of the Jewish nation being freed from Egypt. Reports reached him telling of the greatness of Moses; he was informed that not only was Moses the individual who led the Jewish nation out of slavery, but that he was also the paradigm of personal perfection. He heard that Moses had reached such heights in compassion, in kindness, and moral integrity that God chose him to be the one to receive the prophetic word on Mt. Sinai.

"Being far away, the king sent one of his artists to bring him back a likeness of Moses. When the long awaited portrait arrived, the King sent for his wise men to study the painting. Being schooled in the ancient art of determining a person's nature based on his facial features, they were dumfounded. After studying the portrait of Moses, they told the King, that the picture they were being shown was that of a selfish, egocentric, and mean-spirited person. The King was taken aback. He assumed that either his artist must have taken down an inaccurate impression, or that his wise men were mistaken. He made up his mind to go and visit Moses and decide for himself.

"When he arrived at the encampment of the Jewish People he was greeted with great respect and brought in to see Moses. The King turned to Moses and said, *'Dear sir, I am perplexed, I sent my emissary to paint a portrait of yourself. My wise men who are students of the human character, tell me that based on your outer features you have the nature of a wicked person. Tell me, is it my artist who has erred, or my wise men?'*

"To which Moses answered, *'Both of them are correct. What your wise men perceive is in fact my inner nature. My tendency from birth is to be selfish, cruel, and arrogant. I have spent my life working on these traits until I have eradicated them from my being.'*

"The truly amazing part of this incident is that we are taught that one of the kindest, most compassionate human beings, who ever existed on the face of this planet was Moses. In the Bible, God Himself says about Moses:

"There is none as humble as he amongst man."
(Numbers 12:13)

"Is there any greater accolade that can be bestowed upon a man? At that time he was the sole leader of a nation of 3 million people, all of whom regarded him as a man of God. He was the one that an entire people turned to for direction and guidance. With all of the honor and glory heaped upon him, he is called by God, *'the most humble of all men.'*

"Yet he revealed in that one statement about himself, that his nature, the tendencies with which he was born were far from greatness.

"You see, David, Moses wasn't born great; he made himself into the great man he became. He shaped himself to be what he eventually was. He had the same inclinations and tendencies as any human and according to his own admission, maybe far worse. The question is what he did with it.

"Unfortunately, this is a part of the human dynamics that we pay little attention to—the change that our actions have upon us. Life is actually an arena of opportunities, opportunities to do good or bad; but as importantly, opportunities to shape our very nature. Every time you face a challenge, not only have you won a battle, you have also strengthened yourself, and you are now the better for it, ready for the next level of challenge. Ideally, if a person were to win all of the battles of life, he would go from level to level in a constant growth pattern, until after a lifetime of work, he would reach the ultimate level of perfection. That is the purpose of life.

"Unfortunately we win some and we lose some. When we lose, we set ourselves back, we create obstacles for our further growth, and we make it that much harder to win the next battle. When we win, we set the path for future success.

"The difficult part is that life is so complicated, and the challenges come in so many different shapes and forms. When I have finally gotten one level down, and now understand the right way to approach a given situation, a new one springs up, one that has no correlation to the old. Each of life's circumstances is new and unrelated to the one that came before it.

"And, because we are speaking about the perfection of man—it cuts across all elements of human behavior and interactions—perfection across the full gamut of the human personality; improving the essence, the nature of the person himself. Starting with character traits: Kindness, Compassion, Generosity, Humility, Anger, Jealousy, and Hatred, and encompassing all of the moral issues that a person encounters in life. In each arena the right choice propels us towards growth, and the wrong choice retards our progress. So how can we possibly reach these heights? How can we possibly find our way in the maze of choices, and discover that one golden path that allows us, as individuals, to reach our potential?

"For this God gave us a guidebook, to show us the way, a divinely authored work, to be a guide towards spiritual perfection. Our Creator, Who alone understands the true inner workings of the human, gave us a methodology whereby a person can reach spiritual heights. It is the science and the art behind the perfection of the human. And it contains the formulas and techniques for working on and growing in these areas. God gave us the Torah, the written and oral law to be our guiding light in life. If a person follows its ways, they will grow level after level till they reach great spiritual heights, and in that state live on forever. If they don't they are like a raft out at sea, drifting with each passing wind that blows, never reaching home port, because they don't even know in which direction to sail. The stakes of life are very high; at game is human perfection and eternity. God gave us a program to follow, the greatest system for self perfection. It is our charge to study the Torah and learns its ways, then apply it to our lives."

Chapter 15: Animal Soul / Spiritual Soul

And God created man in his image
(Genesis 3)

"Rabbi," David said, "I can tell you that our sessions are really having an effect."

"In what sense?"

"Well, if nothing else it has gotten to the point that Susan is jealous. She and I spend a good deal of time discussing the issues that we get involved with here, and she keeps mentioning that she feels left out of our discussions."

"Why don't you ask her to join us the next time we meet?" I said. "In the meantime, I have something I would like to share with you. I am sure that you have heard this Biblical verse quoted many times: "*And man was created in the image of God.*" Did you ever wonder what that means? Or let me put it this way, have you ever seen a man create a world, or even a sun for that matter? Have you met a man that has lived for, say, a thousand years? Or one who can control the winds in the sky, or make it rain?"

"I thought that expression didn't mean literally like God," David responded. "I assumed it referred to the Godliness in all men."

"I think that you are right," I said. "However, to clarify what I am getting at, I can recite for you an entire litany of human behaviors that are far from being Godlike. We don't have to look very hard to find men whose behavior seems more easily compared to an animal's, than to God's. So in what sense does the Bible mean that man is created in the image of God?

"To come to an understanding of this issue, we need some background as to what makes up the inner essence of the human being. I would like to read you another excerpt from a book called *Duties of the Heart.* Along with the *Path of the Just*, it rates as one of the prime sources of Jewish thought. Also written long ago, as a guide to life, it as applicable and universally accepted now as it ever was. This is from Section 3, Chapter 2, entitled Serving God:

'Man was created from elements that are very different, whose essence are opposites, and whose very natures are in competition. They are his body and his soul. Within man, God implanted drives and desires that are necessary for the continuation of the human species, these are all of the desires for physical pleasures, they are in man as in all animals. If man makes use of them he will strengthen his physical standing, and the human race will flourish. In addition to these, God implanted within the human soul strengths, which if man uses, will cause him to look down on his position in this world and make him desire to separate from it. This is his spiritual part.'

"Within this short paragraph we have been given the formula for the very nature of man. When God created man, He joined together two diverse elements to make up the soul of man. Part of man's soul is from the highest parts of the cosmos. That part only wants to do what is right and proper. We call that Godlike part, man's <u>Spiritual Soul</u>. The other part of man's soul is very different. It is exactly like that of an animal, with all of the passions and desires necessary to keep him alive; it is his <u>Animal Soul</u>."

David looked at me a little perplexed as he said, "What do you mean by an Animal Soul?"

"An animal also has a living essence," I said. "Just like man, it has a part of it that isn't physical. It has a nature and tendencies; it is attracted toward certain types of objects and repelled by others. A dog will form attachments to its master, and will even risk its own life to defend its owner.

"I remember when I was in school there was a fellow, Fred, who had a problem going home. When he went away to school he had to part with the dog that he grew up with. Since he was a child, this dog had been a part of his life, and there was a real bond between them. It seemed that the separation was harder on the dog than on Fred. Every few months, when Fred would go back home to visit, his dog would run out to greet him. The problem was that at the sight of his master, this dog would get into a frenzy, and in his excitement, relieve itself all over his master's pants leg! I'm not sure Fred was too happy about his pet's loyalty.

"The point is that there is a part of a dog that is alive—we would almost say it has a personality. We don't normally think of animals as having a soul. But they, too, have a part that is vibrant and interactive, and just like a human soul, this part isn't physical, it is a spiritual component. When a dog sleeps, the body lies there flat, almost lifeless, when the dog wakes up, its essence comes back again. That part of the animal, its inner essence, we would call the Animal Soul.

"God implanted into the soul of an animal all of the instincts that it needs for its survival. The cat instinctively seeks out a mouse for its sustenance. The bird naturally hungers for a worm. It would be hard to imagine a hummingbird going through a cognitive process, thinking, *'Based on my nutritional needs, my physical capacity to hunt, capture, and digest such foods, coupled with the general availability of such items, I have surmised that it would be best for me to utilize the worm as my food staple.'* A bird eats worms by instinct. It has a natural pull, an inborn inclination towards worms. It hungers for worms.

"Studies show that animals raised in captivity, upon being released into the wild, will instinctively hunt for the ideal food source of their species. Siberian Tigers, orphaned at birth and brought up on bottled milk, once released, begin hunting deer—their natural food source—even though these tigers had never before seen a deer, let alone witnessed one being hunted down to be eaten. Inborn in their essence is a drive for the types of foods that best facilitates their survival.

"So, too, animals mate. Two Bull Frogs don't go through a thought process of *'I think it's now time for us to settle down and raise a family.'* Rather, God implanted all of the necessary instincts and drives for the survival of the individual animal, as well as the species as a whole, into the animal. That part, the instinctual, hungering part is its Animal Soul.

"Man also has an Animal Soul similar to that found in the animal kingdom. There is a part of him that desires physical things. He desires to eat, sleep, and procreate. There is a part of him that hungers for food. These desires may be awakened by that empty feeling in his stomach, but the craving for eating is there within him. Within the "I" there is a part that desires to procreate. We wouldn't say that a person's body hungers for procreation, rather he does, the essence of him desires it. These are all inclinations that God put into the Animal Soul of man to keep man alive on this planet. If man follows these instincts he will survive, and the species of man will continue. The Animal Soul forms a part of me. The "I" that thinks and feels, is comprised in part of these instincts and drives.

"There is another part of me, the Spiritual Soul. This is the part of me that is considered greater than the angels. This is the part of me that only wants to do what is good and proper. It wishes to be charitable, and giving. It only knows generosity and concern for others. This is the Godlike part of me. It was implanted in me, as it was in every human being. It, too, hungers for things. It, too, instinctively desires things. However, since this component comes from the upper worlds and was created in such purity and perfection, it has needs that are very different from those of the Animal Soul. It craves to do that which is noble and right. It needs to contribute; it needs to do 'good'; it needs to be generous. By its very nature it can't be self serving, it needs to give. This part is holy and pure. It doesn't know how to ask for itself, it is always concerned with doing for others. It wants to help, it feels other's pain and wishes that it could do something to lighten their load. This is the part of me that is pure goodness, and only wants to do what is proper and elevated in life.

"It is also the component in me that isn't satisfied with the physical, mundane existence that I lead. It screams out for something more meaningful, something deeper and more significant. It is that part of me that deeply needs to do something of consequence and substance—to make a lasting contribution. When God created man, it was this part that He referred to as the greatness of man. It is this element that is pure and holy. It is this component in me that it was worth creating heaven and earth for. This part is the true greatness of man.

"The "I" that am thinking right now, the "I" that feels and plans, is comprised of both of these parts. I am both animal instincts and pure spirituality. I have a part of me that is instinctive much like any member of the animal kingdom. When a dog feels a need to procreate there is nothing that stops it; desire rules over the animal. I have that side to me as well. I have within me a set of inborn instincts that hungers for physical activities and pursuits. The greatness of the human is that there is the other part of me that is pure spirit and goodness, that can control the animal instincts. It can use those drives and passions properly, channeling them to productive and positive ends.

"Because my Spiritual Soul is from the upper worlds it enjoys very little of this world. When I am out there on a Sunday afternoon mowing the lawn, this part of me is getting very little pleasure. This is the part that won't let me rest. It is always demanding, relentlessly requiring that I grow; that I accomplish; that I do something significant with my time. This side drives everything great and noble in the human. Anything that you ever hear about the greatness of man stems from this side. This is what propels the person to heights, if he follows it correctly.

"David," I said, "do you remember when we spoke about that Voice Inside, that part of us that intuitively knows right from wrong? That voice is this spiritual part of us. What we might call in vague terms a conscience, or a sense of propriety, is the voice of the Spiritual Soul. All of the higher values that we find intuitive to a person stem from this side. When we find an instinctive sense of the value of a human life; when we look at medical personnel who go to any length to save a human; it is because they were preprogrammed with this understanding, as all humans are. They were born with this side of their soul that is perfect and understands the value of life. When we find successful people with good careers at the top of their game who just aren't happy, they aren't satisfied, it is because this part of them, their Spiritual Soul isn't being nourished. This Spiritual Soul is the Voice Inside that drives you to do 'good' and won't let you rest when you have done something wrong. When it feels that you have done something that is improper it keeps welling up inside you and sermonizes. It lectures, and it won't stop. It keeps on and on. And you can't run from it, because it is you.

"This part is the height of the human. If man would only listen to that voice, mankind would have long ago reached a state of perfection. We would be living in a utopian society, everyone would only be concerned for the good of others, there would be no greed or avarice, there would only be charity and loving kindness in the world. However, we also have this other component that only knows its own needs and desires. By its very nature the Animal Soul can only think of its own needs. It can't give, it is incapable of sacrificing; it only knows and exists for its own fulfillment.

"These two elements of man are opposites and are actually fighting for primacy in each person. As a result, man is in constant flux. The very purpose of creation is to allow one or the other to become the controlling force over the person. The more a person uses one element, the stronger and more influential it becomes over the person. Much like a muscle that with use becomes stronger and with disuse atrophies. If a person uses his Spiritual Soul to control his Animal Soul, then in this battle for primacy it becomes stronger, and the person becomes elevated. If he merely gives in to desires, then the Animal Soul becomes more in control. Not only in a sense of the person acting on his animal instincts, but the person himself becomes more controlled by his drives. His desires become more intense and frequent. They demand to be fulfilled more often, and are more pronounced. In this sense man's Animal Soul is different then that of an animal's. An animal has a set level to its desires. At birth they are fixed in intensity. They will fluctuate based on seasons and circumstances, but all within a given range. Man, on the other hand, has less restriction on the range of intensity. If he controls his animal instincts they lessen and it becomes easier for him to dominate over them. If he allows them to rule over him, they become stronger and more extreme until they are much more difficult to restrain.

"You see, David: we humans are preprogrammed for greatness. We have this part of us that is hardwired to do only good, to be great and accomplish grand things on this planet. We are also equipped with a part of us that has no intelligence whatsoever, that only manifests itself as hungers and desires. We are here on this planet in the process of shaping our very selves. As we discussed, each of our character traits is moldable. So, too this balance within us is constantly being affected by our thoughts, words and actions. The essence of who I am, and who I will be for eternity is based on choices of which side I listen to and allow to come to the fore.

See Diagram II on Page 104

"The process of living is actually a battle between these two forces. Ideally, if a person succeeded completely, his pure intellectual soul would harness his Animal Soul and use it for the purpose of keeping himself alive. Like a Captain steering his ship by the wind, he would use the Animal Soul for his objectives—harnessing it, controlling it. By doing so not only does he increase the control that his Godlike part has over him, but he elevates everything that he does. When he eats, it is for the purpose of being strong, so that he can properly perform his mission on this planet. When he procreates; it is for the purpose of bringing children into the world, and creating a harmonious, loving marriage. The pleasures that he takes from this world are for a purpose, so that he should be happy and better suited to pursue his path. In this manner, mundane physical activities, necessary for human survival, are elevated to the highest forms of positive acts, and the human functions on the highest level of spirituality—an angel in the form of a man.

Implanted in the human at birth is an Animal Soul and a Spiritual Soul. Each has a different nature and tendency. The stronger the Animal Soul becomes the more influence it exerts over the "I", the stronger the Spiritual Soul becomes the more influence it exerts over the "I". During life, the two are in constant flux, with one or the other gaining primacy.

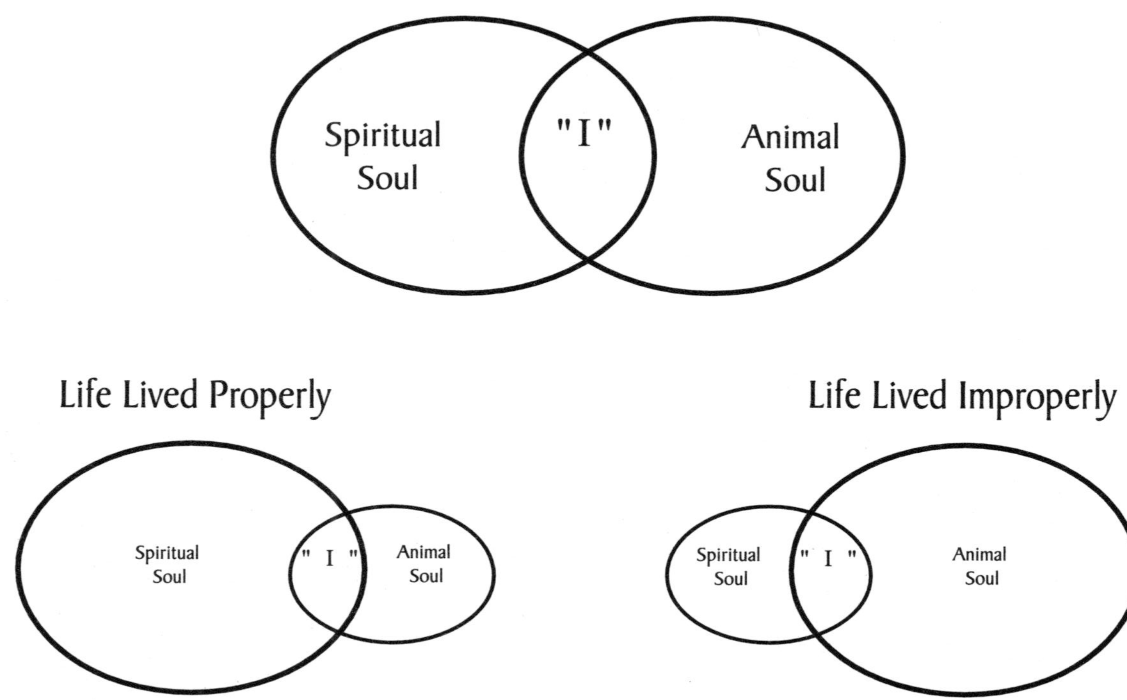

"On the other hand, if a man allows his animal desires to win out and follows their natural pull without controlling them, they become stronger and more controlling over his personality. His desires become stronger and start to rule over him. He is no longer able to make sound decisions. Rather, like an animal he reacts by inclinations and desires. He is ruled over by whims and passions, until he loses control of himself and ultimately the ability to even choose. He becomes more animal like and less God like; until he becomes an animal in the shape of a man.

"This is the human—a walking, breathing, living contradiction; because we have been created from two such different parts, so opposite in nature. Do you ever wonder how it is that we can find the same individual acting in such opposite manners? On one occasion acting benevolent and kindly, yet the same person in a similar situation acting in the most selfish, self centered, petty manner? That person isn't some freak, some Dr. Jeckle and Mr. Hyde—It is me! Catch me at the right moment, in the right situation, and I can act like the most noble, distinguished person you could ever want to meet. And I, the very same person, will act so small and petty the next moment. It is because my inner essence is in complete contradiction. I am made up of these two competing, complete opposites.

"You see, David, we are often too kind to ourselves, we don't spend any where near enough energy watching ourselves and seeing who we really are. We are so accustomed to making excuses and explaining away our behavior in a favorable light, that we lose the ability to see ourselves with any honest appraisal. But, the reality is that we have two sides, and depending on when you catch us, in what mood we are in, or how the person said what they said to us, our reactions will vary extremely.

"I could be sitting with someone in my study having an inspiring discussion about the greatness of the human spirit, about elevating one's life, and the finest niceties in human behavior; we might go on for hours on end. Later on, I could find out that this man went home, got into a fight with his wife, started swearing, screaming and much worse. I want to ask myself: is that the same man? Is that the same person who just hours ago was involved in a discussion about the betterment of man? Is that the same human being who just condemned violence in society, and then went home and beat his wife?

"We may use such terms as: 'he lost his temper,' or 'he got carried away.' While they are certainly correct, these living contradictions are indicative of more going on underneath the surface of the person. They are a result of our being formed from these two rival elements. When one side has primacy, we can be kind, sweet and considerate; when the other side gets in control, then watch out. The same person, a different mood, a different setting, and we are witnessing diametrically opposed behavior.

"You open a paper and see another auto accident tied to road rage. The Buick® cuts off the Chevy®. In an act of vengeance the Chevy® chases the Buick® for ten miles finally catching up with it at an intersection, careening into it and injuring five people. Is this the act of a reckless teenager who needs to assert his masculinity? As it turns out the drivers of both cars are over fifty! I just saw a sign on the highway: 'STOP ROAD RAGE, ACT YOUR AGE.' How do we explain mature, sophisticated people acting in a manner so unbecoming to their station in life? Could you imagine their embarrassment if, when they were about to pull across the other vehicle, they saw the driver is someone they know? How about if it's their boss? They would be deadly embarrassed, because they were acting like a ten year old throwing a temper tantrum. Yet this is so common that it has become an epidemic on our roads. How do we explain such a phenomena?

"How do we explain very driven people, powerful goal setters, extremely successful at what they do, throwing away everything they have, their career, their marriage, their reputation, all for a fling with a secretary? If we claim to understand the very fabric of the human personality, how do we make sense of these happenings?

The answer is, that after giving in to these desires man loses control. He becomes more animal-like, being ruled over by desires and passions. Animals react—they have instincts and desires that cause them to act. An animal can't control itself. When the desire to mate hits it, there is no Free

Will. There is no controlling agent that will hold it back. Anyone who has ever owned a pet in heat will tell you stories of cats, jumping through plate glass windows, and of dogs, digging holes under a garden fence, because the animal is captivated by an uncontrollable urge.

"Man starts out in a very different state. He, too, has urges and desires, but he has the capacity to control and harness them. If man does this and follows a proper course of life, then these drives and desires, while still a part of him, become less powerful. They lessen in intensity and in the urgency with which they demand being fulfilled. When man gives in to these passions without controlling them, he effectively gives up control over himself. They grow and become more demanding, more incessant and more potent, exerting more pull and control over him. They begin affecting his judgments and decisions, exerting more and more influence and rule over him—they become the master and he the slave. Until he reaches a point where he does things that he never would have done in his right mind, things that are destructive to him and completely against his self interest. Throughout the process he may think that he maintains control, but like a drug addict who needs a fix, the urge becomes so strong and demanding that it would take superhuman effort to resist it. The desire didn't start that strong. At an earlier stage in his life it didn't envelope him to the extent that it does now. It was a long process of 'giving in' that allowed these desires to become stronger, causing him to slowly lose more and more control of himself, until he finds himself in a position, where he may be almost incapable of controlling himself.

"So we are this contradictory combination. These two total opposites put together, forged to create this whole we know as the human; each part crying out for its fulfillment; each component vying for control and the human is in a state of constant change with one or the other gaining primacy. Is it any wonder that we find such varied and diverse behavior from a being whose very natures are at odds?

"The challenge of life is to perfect ourselves by finding the path that brings about our growth, and allows our instinctive desire to do what is right and noble to win out. The choices that I make shape the very person that I am. The difficult part is that it is "I", who is in contradiction. It is "I" that wants to grow; and the very same "I" that wants to mire in the mud. It is "I" that wishes to shoot for the stars, to reach the heights of humanity, and it is "I" that is satisfied to go on living without a plan, without direction just taking life as it comes.

"To allow man to succeed, God gave us a method that will allow that part of us that is great to come to the fore. He gave us a program for spiritual development, the system for accomplishing that which we were put on this planet for. That system is the Torah, the God given written and oral law given to the Jewish people on Mount Sinai.

"The Torah provides us with guidelines and a system that allows all that is great in the human to come to the fore. It is the program that allows the spiritual part of man to grow and dominate the Animal Soul within him. The Torah is replete with commandments and actions many of whose meanings are readily understood, others that take greater depth to understand. All focus is on this one goal, to strengthen man's spiritual side, to allow it to come forward, and gain primacy. It is the pathway that will allow that part of me that is great, that part of me that has the potential to be greater than the angels, to come to the fore, and allow me to reach the heights of greatness which I was predestined for.

"Why don't we stop here? And please invite Susan to join us next week."

Chapter 16: Pants Too Short Syndrome

When Susan and David walked in, I couldn't help but notice what a handsome couple they were, both tall, well dressed with such an air of confidence about them.

"Hi! So you must be Susan," I said. "It's a pleasure to meet you. I've heard so much about you. Please have a seat."

"Hi," Susan answered. "David has told me a lot about you as well. Rabbi," she said as she sat down, "it's a little awkward finally meeting you. I feel like a kid who used to stand outside the stadium while the game was on, listening for the cheer of the crowds, to see who wins."

"In what sense?" I said

"You and David have been meeting for a while now, and while I get to hear much of the content, it comes to me second hand; I never got to actually be a part of the discussions. I feel that much of what you have been speaking about are areas that I haven't properly explored myself, and to be honest, I've been having trouble with some of the ideas."

"What particular area is troubling you?" I asked.

"I don't know how much David has told you about my background, but I grew up knowing very little about Judaism. In my heart I always knew that I was a Jew, but as far as actual practice I had no involvement. When I was younger, my parents sent me to Sunday school, but I found the whole experience empty—I just didn't feel anything. Even my Bat Mitzvah didn't feel like a religious experience, it was more like a party.

"Once I went away for college I didn't even attend services on Yom Kippur."

"What changed?" I asked.

"That's kind of an interesting subject. For me it wasn't like some kind of spiritual awakening or even a philosophical one, it was more of a family thing. It started when I was a Junior in college. One of my roommates was a very religious girl, she ate only Kosher, and wouldn't turn lights on or off on the Sabbath. Often we would get into discussions about the meaning of these things, but they had little impact on me until she invited me to her house for the Sabbath. She would go home every weekend, and her whole family would get together. I had never been to a formal Sabbath meal, so I was a little apprehensive—I really didn't know what to expect.

"At first I turned her down, but she kept asking me, so finally I said yes. What I saw blew me away! She was the oldest of six children. Here they were, her mother, father, grandmother, grandfather, and all the children, sitting around the table, all dressed in their finest clothing, all speaking the same language, all with a common bond. During the meal, the discussions were lively, focused and meaningful; I felt such a calm unity in what they were doing. I had never experienced anything like this before.

"What struck me more than anything was the children, they were so respectful—especially the way they interacted with their grandparents. I know this may sound obvious, but they actually respected them. It wasn't like some kind of "let's humor the old folks". They were really listening and wanted to hear what their elders had to say. I thought of my own upbringing in comparison, and how different it was; how disconnected I was to my own family. I realized there had to be something to this.

"So I began studying about Judaism. I went often to their house, and pretty soon I began attending synagogue on the Sabbath. I met other families, all with the same strong attachment, and before you knew it I became a part of the community. I just fell into a way of life that I saw as so wholesome, and I wanted to be a part of it, I wanted to raise my own family that way. Granted, I learned about the traditions and customs, and

I began seeing the beauty in them; I felt part of this heritage going back 3,000 years, but the main thing that attracted me was the concept of the family connected through a common bond. I guess you could call me a social Jew."

"That's great," I responded. "There is no question that family plays an essential role in our religion, and the focus of much of what we do revolves around keeping a proper balance in our life. So what is the problem?"

"Well, it seems to me that much of your discussions with David are based on a premise that all of the Mitzvahs are vehicles to perfect man, and that, in fact, the whole reason we were created was to allow us to grow, so that, for eternity, we can enjoy that which we have accomplished; that God created us *'not for our place in this world, but rather for our place in the world to come...'* Am I on track?"

"Yes," I said, "I think that is an accurate synopsis of our discussions."

"Rabbi..." and now Susan hesitated, as if what she was going to say was something she was almost afraid to ask.

"It seems that you have something on your mind," I said.

"I do. But I'm not sure that I should be asking it."

"There is only one way to tell: ask and we'll find out."

"I mean... I know that we are supposed to have faith, and I certainly appreciate how much time you have been spending with David... I'm just not sure whether this issue that is troubling me is something we need to take on faith?"

"Susan, even before you start, let me give you some background. When you say faith, I assume that you mean a sort of vague uncertainty that will never be cleared up; as if belief and faith means just accepting things when you're really not sure. That type of faith has little to do with the practice of Judaism.

"Let me show you what I mean. I was once having a discussion with an older woman, who came to the synagogue on Rosh Hashanah. She told me that she found the experience horribly boring.

"She continued to fast on Yom Kippur and go to services even though she saw no meaning in it. In the course of conversation I mentioned to her, that not only do I pray on holidays and the Sabbath, but three times each day as well. At which point she said to me, *'Rabbi I guess it is just a matter of faith, you have more faith than I do.'*

"Susan, in retrospect I agree with her, it is a matter of faith. But it is she, who has far more faith than I. You see, for me to pray or to observe the rituals of Judaism fundamentally makes sense. It is something that fits into a pattern of service of God and self perfection. I understand their effect and I relate to them as powerfully constructive and meaningful acts—so it doesn't take that much faith for me to do these things. But this woman was continuing to do something that made no sense to her: she continued to go to services on Rosh Hashanah even though to her this was a mindless activity; she continued to fast on Yom Kippur even though she didn't see the purpose of it. She did these things for only one reason; because her parents did them before her—that takes great faith.

"In Judaism, we do very little based on that kind of faith, which really translates as 'just accepting things.' Our belief system and all that we do both in terms of commandments and customs is based on **knowledge**—not faith. The whole process of studying Torah and becoming more familiar with the Mitzvahs is one of questioning and understanding. It takes a while to gain the complete picture, until the significance of everything fits into a larger picture, and so we may begin by doing things that we don't yet fully fathom, but the basis of it all, and the end goal is understanding. So, please go ahead, ask whatever is on your mind."

"OK," Susan said, "here is the point. I now consider myself a religious person. For the past number of years I have been studying about Judaism, and keeping the Mitzvahs, yet I haven't even thought in these terms. I agree that this idea of a person needing a purpose in life makes a lot of sense, but it seems that the religion would stand without it. All of the rituals would have their place, the Torah study would help us be more moral and better people, and each of the holidays would have its special message. So how do you know that these theories are right? I don't mean it in a disrespectful manner, but how do you know that your way of looking at life, and our purpose in being here, is correct?"

"That certainly is a fair question," I answered. "How does any human being, who is here today and gone tomorrow, who passes his life like a puff of smoke, have the audacity to think that he has a world view that addresses the very essence, the purpose of life? That would be sheer arrogance and maybe even stupidity. For that reason, I agree that had our discussions been based on my opinions, my thoughts, and my conclusions, then we would be on shaky ground. After all, how do I know that I am correct? How could I sit down and offer you what I feel is a course by which to lead your life, when in fact it may be dead wrong?

"That's why I want to make one point: this isn't my view. This isn't my theology or brand of religion. What we are speaking about is part of the Torah: the Written Law and Oral Tradition given by God to Moses and the Jewish Nation at Mt. Sinai. These are teachings that were transmitted by our forefathers dating back more than 3,000 years, without changes and without deviations. These are eternal words of truth that have been handed down parent to child, scholar to student, generation to generation in an unbroken chain of oral transmission, emanating from God Himself.

"This isn't the world according to Rabbi X, to be argued with by Rabbi Y, to be refuted by Rabbi Z. What we have been talking about are fundamental tenets of Judaism. All part of the Torah written by God Himself, handed down era to era. As such it was taught, studied, and reviewed, without changes or modifications; as a guide to life and our road map for living."

David looked at me and said, "That's part of the problem. You are saying, that the Bible, or the Torah, is our guide to living life now?"

"Exactly."

David looked pained as he said, "I can't say that I ever articulated this, but in the back of my mind I always looked at the Bible as sort of... well kind of like a book of stories. I'm sure they are all meaningful and instructive, but in terms of being a guiding light for our lives now... I mean, I find it hard to see how stories about building an ark, or about Moses going to King Pharaoh have much relevance to my life."

"David," I said. "You aren't the first person to bring up this point. I am often amazed when I find myself speaking with sophisticated, intelligent people, who understand the vastness and complexity of the world in which we live. We may even enter into discussions about the extraordinary wisdom that is manifest in every facet of the world, and we have no problem taking the next step: recognizing that all of this was created by God. There was nothing, and then with words alone, God created this entire phenomenally complex world that we live in. There was no such entity as light, and God said: *'Let there be light,'* and light came into being; with all of the power, properties and intricate laws of quantum physics. There was no such thing as matter, and God said: *'Let there be,'* and all of the laws of matter and physics came into being. All of the vast wisdom and sheer wonder of this world, that after millenniums of discovery, man has only begun to scratch the surface of understanding, was brought into existence by God with words alone.

"Yet these very same people, who fully appreciate all of the wisdom manifested in creation, look at this guidebook written by the Creator as a kind of simple book written for primitives, with no real relevance to us today. As if the Creator, whose wisdom is so clearly visible in everything that He made, set out to write a work containing the secrets of life, and couldn't do any better then write a book of simple Bible stories. Sort of makes you wonder, doesn't it?

"I have a feeling that the reason that people may look at the Torah as a book of simple stories is because they fall prey to what I call the *'Pants Too Short Syndrome.'* Here's what it's about. If you go to a Synagogue on a major Jewish holiday, look around at the young men who are almost fourteen years old. You will find at least one of them whose pants legs end somewhere between his ankles and his knees (often times closer to his knees).

"What happened was that this young man had his Bar Mitzvah sometime that year. In honor of the event he went with his mother to get a new suit, and they had it tailored—a perfect fit. After the Bar Mitzvah when all the aunts, uncles, cousins and friends went home, this young man put away his new suit. It is now six months later, for an occasion such as Passover it is fitting for him to wear his Bar Mitzvah suit. So he pulls it out of the closet and proudly wears it to synagogue. He forgot one point: he grew a lot since his Bar Mitzvah, and the suit no longer fits. So he shows up at the Synagogue looking like the great flood just hit!

"For a lot of people this example is comparable to their knowledge of Torah. They had some instruction in Bible when they were young. Maybe they went to Sunday school and that was it, they haven't been involved since then, so their knowledge of the Bible has stopped at the comprehension level of a ten or twelve year old. They are now mature adults, dealing with real life issues: questions of meaning in life, moral dilemmas, and difficult life decisions. What bearing does a third grade understanding of the Torah have on these mature issues? The understanding that they were capable of absorbing at that age is where they left off; of course it has no relevance to their life now as a mature person. It is like putting a child's suit on an adult—it doesn't fit.

"I think this is a large part of the reason that some of our own youth, when searching for spirituality, go to other religions, not even being aware of the meaning, depth and profundity contained in the Torah, given to us by God.

"The only solution is to begin a study of it now, as mature adults—to discover the depth contained within it, and find its relevance to our lives. When God gave us this work it wasn't meant for the people of those times—it was given for eternity, to be the guidebook for the generations.

It was to be eternally relevant and eternally fitting, to be as much a force in our lives now, as it was a thousand years ago; as it will be a thousand years from now.

"Some things change, but the meaning and purpose of life doesn't change. So, too, the system for man to lead a happy, prosperous life, and to find fulfillment in this world doesn't change. These were given to man by God in a format to be transmitted through the epochs. This system for human perfection, this guidebook for life, is the same Torah that we have studied without change; without it being watered down to fit the norms of current times, for millennia now. It is timeless and unchanged having been so designed by the Master of the Universe, God Himself."

David sat there for a while, lost in thought and finally said: "Rabbi, I hear your point that the only possible source that one could rely on for the ultimate truth would have to authored by God—and you say that the Torah is that book. That brings me to another issue that I never really got clear. I never thought of the Bible as having been written by God. I always assumed that the Greeks have their mythology, the Romans have their Gods, and we have our collection of legends and parables, collected by wise men to aid us in living a more ethical life. How do you know that the Bible was written by God?"

Chapter 17: Torah From Sinai

"David," I said, "you are certainly raising a valid concern, one that will shape the entire course of our discussions. If your assumption is right, that the Torah is a collection of stories, maybe even a code of ethics compiled by wise men of previous generations, then, while it may rank as a significant piece of literature, we certainly can't give it too much weight. However, if it were written by God Himself then the value of it is immeasurable."

"I agree," David answered. "But, that is the key question, whether, in fact, it was written by God or not."

"OK," I said, "let's see whether there is any proof to the Torah having been given by God."

"The Kuzari, one of the great works on Jewish thought, written in the 11th century, makes an important observation. One of the points that distinguishes Judaism from other religions is the claim upon which it is based. Every religion starts with one man having a dream or a religious experience. It might be backed up by a tight knit band of his disciples seeing a miracle, but in the end, it is based on an event that is easy to falsify and difficult to substantiate—maybe it did occur as we are told, maybe it didn't. It may well have been a design to gain support for what one man thought would be a higher ideal, and we have no way of verifying that the event ever happened.

"Judaism's claim is that a people, an entire nation, witnessed God speaking to them. An entire huge assemblage heard God telling them the Ten Commandments, instructing them in the basis of belief. This is a claim that is impossible to falsify and easy to substantiate.

"In Exodus Chapter 19 and 20, the Bible describes the giving of the Torah.

"And God spoke to Moses, saying, 'I will appear to you in the thickness of cloud, so that the nation should hear me speak to you, and so that they will trust in you forever. Tell the nation to prepare for three days, for on the third day, God will appear to the entire nation, on Mt. Sinai.'

"The verses tell us that the entire nation of Israel was gathered at Mt. Sinai, when God Himself spoke to them.

"Now, let's think about this, this event is three months after the Jewish nation has been taken out of Egypt. The bible also tells us that at the Exodus there were 600,000 men between the age of twenty and sixty. If you add the women, we are now dealing with a group of 1.2 million. Add those older than sixty and younger than twenty and you have at least three million people witnessing an event. The claim that Judaism makes is that God appeared to the Jewish nation in the most public manner imaginable. The question is, can something that public be falsified?

"David, did you ever hear the expression: *'Ask two Jews, you'll get three opinions?'* We seem to be a very opinionated people. From the moment of the giving of the Torah on Mt. Sinai till today, we are a questioning people, we don't merely accept things. The Bible itself calls us a stiff-necked people. The Jewish nation spent forty years in the desert, being prepared to enter the land of Israel. We now have this glorified view that everyone during this time period obeyed the word of God dutifully. While it is true that the nation on the whole was on an exalted level, there was quite a bit of dissension, particularly against Moses as the leader.

"There were those among the Jewish nation who were jealous of Moses, as he now occupied the throne of glory. He was chosen to be the one to go up to heaven and bring down the law from God himself. He was now the teacher of the nation, and this brought resentment and caused jealousy. On a number of occasions the Torah tells us that groups formed to oppose Moses. Every time that Moses made the slightest move that left him open, they attacked him. When there was no water, there was dissension against Moses. When the people were tired of eating Manna, there was opposition. When God told him to appoint his brother Aaron as the high priest, Korach and his people staged an outright revolution against Moses.

"Keeping this in mind, I have an observation to make: the Torah and the study of the Torah were central to the Jewish people in the desert; the main activity during the forty years spent wandering was studying the Torah. This time was to be used as a spiritual growth period for the Jewish People; an interval for increasing knowledge and understanding of the Torah. The custom that we keep till this day of reading the weekly portion of the Torah on the Sabbath was begun by Moses himself, in the desert. So I have one simple question to ask. Why didn't someone come along and question this entire story of the giving of the Torah on Mt. Sinai? If there was any slight inaccuracy of any sort, when they were reading about the events, someone should have gotten up, and said: *'Hey, this stuff just didn't happen, I was there, and it never occurred.'*

At this point Susan interjected, "Rabbi, that doesn't prove anything, in fact, it's almost circular logic. If, in fact, these events were read about in the weekly Bible portion, from the time the Jews were in the desert till now, then what you are saying is consistent. How do we know that it ever happened? Maybe the entire Bible was something that came about centuries later. Maybe the Rabbis a thousand years ago introduced the entire work."

"Susan," I said, "to properly answer this question we have to deal with the central role that the Torah has played in our nation. To our people the Torah isn't some obscure law book, stored away to be read only by scholars. For thousands of years it has been the heart blood of our people. Wherever we went, in whichever country we were exiled, the Torah and its study came with us. From antiquity, we are known as the people of the book, long before there was a printing press, long before books were something found in every person's home, we acquired that accolade. Our reputation was one of a studious people, and throughout history what we studied was the Torah. Every Jewish child began his education with the Torah and continued this study throughout his life. As it is read weekly in our synagogues it has been read for 3,300 years, read, studied, discussed, and analyzed—the Torah has been the center of Jewish life throughout the ages. It was taught mother to daughter, teacher to student, in an unending tradition. How do you falsify such a document?"

"Rabbi," Susan said, "again, I don't mean to be argumentative. But, let's say that twelve hundred years ago the Rabbis got together and reached the conclusion that the faith is weakening and they must do something about it, so they made certain inclusions in the Bible itself, they added certain parts, changed certain segments, keeping the majority, but changing some events."

"Here is the problem with that theory," I responded. "How come nobody screamed?"

"Let's imagine you had been studying a Shakespearean text for thirty years. You had performed the play many times, you taught it on a college level, maybe you even authored a commentary on it. Along comes a group of professors saying:

'Ladies and gentlemen, we wish to make some changes. To allow the plays to have greater social relevance, and be more politically correct, we are going to change things a little bit. So now, instead of Shylock crying out for his pound of flesh, he will accept a note payable in five years. Hamlet is going to conduct a popularity poll before any major decision. And, when Juliet cries out to Romeo to join her, he will respond: 'Since I am confined to a wheel chair, and am blind in both eyes, I am unable to join you my dear.' How easy a time do you think they would have pulling it off?

"Susan, keep in mind that Shakespeare's plays are but one of thousands of literary works. Most people read them once or twice and then put them down to gather dust on a shelf, and yet it would be absurd for someone to make those kinds of changes and hope to get away with it. Do you remember when they introduced new Coke®, there was such an uproar; demonstrations, protests, and town meetings, you would have thought they were changing the formula of mother's milk. That was just a soft drink. How much more intense would the uproar be, if someone would have tried to change something so fundamental to the Jewish people?

"The Torah has been central to the Jews since they left Egypt. It has been the center of discussions of learning, of lectures and of scholarly works. It was the treasure of the scholar and the lay man alike. We now attend colleges and universities, but for millenniums the sole source of intellectual stimulation for the Jewish people had been the study of the Torah. This was our higher education. Individuals, families, and communities were involved in its study. The mark of the man and his standing at home and in the community was based on his Torah knowledge and scholarship.

"Over 2,000 years ago, in the time of King Chizkiayu, there was a survey done in the land of Israel and the surveyors couldn't find a school age child, who wasn't fluent in the complex laws of spiritual impurity. In the middle ages, the great Maimodimies complained about the common people in his time who devoted only three hours a day to the study of the Torah. He wasn't complaining about the scholars, he was writing about simple workers, regular members of the Jewish People, and Maimodimies was complaining that they weren't diligent enough in their Torah studies, because they only set aside a few hours a day for study!

"In Eastern Europe before WWII, the simplest craftsmen prided themselves on their knowledge of the Torah. Each town had its house of study. Larger towns had separate houses of study divided by profession; there was the tailor's house of study, the shoemaker's house of study, and a separate one for the blacksmiths. The Torah was the pride and joy of our nation, in it we found mental stimulation; in it we found our heritage; and in it we found our connection to God. It was the one golden heritage that parents gave over to their children. Who could possibly introduce a change in something so central to a people, and hope to get away with it?

"What makes this idea even less tenable is the very method that is employed in the study of the Torah. To illustrate this point, I want to share a personal story with you. After I completed high school, I went to study in Israel for a year. There I decided to return to the US and attend a Rabbinical Seminary. I enrolled at one of the major seminaries in NYC, headed by a world famous Torah sage.

"The first week I was there, the head of the seminary gave a lecture, and some of the senior students were standing around afterwards discussing points raised in the dissertation. It sounded like a heated debate, so I walked over to listen. I couldn't call it a discussion, it was really a battle, they were tearing apart the lecture that we had just listened to. *'How do you know?' 'Maybe it could be this way.' 'You have no proof.'* Point, counter point. Point, counter point. Jab, duck, jab, duck, counter punch. A number of the students defending the lecture, others attacking it; back and forth, the speed of the arguments, and the power of the reasoning was amazing, it was something that I had never experienced before. For me it was one of those seminal points that finally hit me: the study of the Torah, specifically the Talmud, is an extraordinarily intense, rigorous mental process, where nothing is taken for granted.

"The Talmud is all about logic, logic that leaves no room for assumptions, no room for lazy thinking, no room to say, *'Well it must make sense, or the Rabbi's of the Talmud never would have accepted it.'* Rather, it is a most demanding, critically honest, procedure of analysis, through the process of questions and answers. *'How do you know?' 'Maybe it is the opposite?' 'What is your proof?'* Questions, questions, questions, and then finally some more questions all focused at arriving at the truth.

"It is considered a true mark of honor if a student can ask a question that forces a Torah scholar to change his position. If a Senior Rabbi is giving a lecture and one of the Students is able to posit an argument that threatens the thesis being presented, his name goes up as one of the rising stars. Torah study is the ultimate process of questioning and probing, descending to the depth of human understanding, the goal being irrefutable, absolute truth. Always looking to unearth the hidden meaning, always looking to uncover the thought process behind the position, and always asking questions; nothing is taken on faith, nothing is taken for granted.

"I often wonder what the scene would look like, if a Catholic Priest were to walk into one of our Rabbinical seminaries. I imagine that he would walk to the back of the study hall, to observe what goes on there. He would hear discussions, arguments, positions refuted, alternatives offered; but most of all questions, questions and more questions. *'How do you know?' 'What is your proof' 'Maybe it is the opposite?'*

"Not just to peers, to teachers, to Senior Rabbi's, to the head of the Seminary. No one is sacred, no one is protected—questions, questions and more questions. *'How do you know?' 'Who told you?' 'Maybe it is the opposite?'* I think the Priest would faint.

"I would expect him to blurt out, *'What is all this questioning, probing, and more questioning, just accept the answer, have faith. The head Rabbi said this is the way it is, just accept it. Just believe!'* I would expect him to walk out muttering something like, *'They have no faith.'*

"Susan, he would be right, but it isn't that we don't have faith, it is that Torah study revolves around understanding, straining our mind to the ultimate level until we are able to grasp things on a deeper and more sophisticated level. It is the ultimate system of comprehension.

"Judaism isn't based on blind faith, it is based on understanding. Understanding life, understanding what our Creator wants from us. Understanding the commandments and how they function. Why they have to be done in a specific manner, and not in some other way. While it is true that each word of the Torah is accepted as absolute truth, as it is the word of God, and emanated from Him on Mt. Sinai, our job is to understand the word, to delve down into its depths. The Torah was given to us to explore, to probe, to grasp as deeply as we are able. There is no faith here; there is deep fundamental knowledge, intellectual probing to the maximum depth of our understanding.

"So, just for the fun of it, let's imagine there is this meeting of the Rabbis, as you put it, there is a decision to change things, to put some things in, take others out. A vote is held and all of the Rabbis agree. Each one goes back to his home town to spread the word. Each Rabbi would then gather together his town, the sages and scholars, the lay men who are adept at Torah studies as well as the more simple laborers, and he would begin the new Gospel.

"We would expect him to say something like:

'There has been a new revelation. Things are different now.'

"What do you think the reaction of the crowd would be? These are the ones who were trained from the cradle to analyze, to scrutinize, and to probe. Since childhood they have been accepting nothing, taking nothing for granted, always questioning and demanding proof. No one is beyond debate; no one is beyond reproach.

"Now, along comes the Rabbi with a new Gospel, a new revelation:

'My friends, things are different, very different, the old is out, and now there is a new. The very basis of our belief system has changed. We must all accept these new thoughts, without asking, without questioning. What is more, from now on we must accept that the old way never happened, it was always this way. When we teach our children we must forget all of the old assumptions, we must teach them this new way only, and we must teach them not to ask about it. Because the council of Rabbis has decided that this is the best way to guarantee Jewish continuity.'

"What do you think the reaction would be? You see, Susan, the very nature of Torah study, by its analysis and striving for truth, doesn't allow for someone to come along and change what we have received on Mt. Sinai. The very system of transmission and the intellectual rigor doesn't allow for falsification.

"When the Jews from Yemen came to Israel in the 1950s, they brought with them their Torah scrolls. This was a part of our people that had been isolated for well over a thousand years, for all of that time there had been no known contact between that community and the rest of the Jewish population. Needless to say, there was great curiosity to see the differences between the Torah scrolls in Israel currently, and the ones that had just been brought in. When they compared the Yemenite Torah Scrolls to the other Torah Scrolls in Israel, ones that had come from Germany, Poland, and Russia, in all the scrolls there was only one letter in one word that was different, (the pronunciation of the two words was the same, it was only a question of spelling).

"Keep in mind that Torah scrolls are hand written, there were no photocopies or printing plates, a scribe sits down to write a scroll, taking as much as a year to complete the task. Yet there was only one letter in the entire work that was different from the ones that came from communities that had been separated for centuries! One letter in one word. One Torah scroll copied from another, generation after generation, over a span of more than a thousand years, and there is less deviation than even a word. Even though there was no cross referencing, no way of checking, and certainly no computer programs that we have now to verify accuracy; yet the transmission was so reliable that it remained perfect and intact. The reason for this is that the Torah plays such an important role to our people, and the exactness of every word is part of the tradition that we have from Mt. Sinai.

"David, we live in a country that is slightly over two hundred years old. Ask any school age child how this nation came about, and he will recount the entire story of the War of Independence. How do we know that England really taxed the colonies without offering them representation? How do we know that there was a Revolutionary War? Maybe it was just propaganda created in the Cold War era, to glorify the founding fathers of our country, and to bolster democratic ideology against the onslaught of Communism?

"The real answer to this is that when something is so public you can't suppress it—the word gets out. People tell people, who chronicle it and write it down. Articles are written, books are published; and the truth is known. When the same report comes from so many different sources, and they all say the same thing, there is no room for error. One person may make up a story, ten people might embellish it, but when you have thousands upon thousands of eye witnesses to an event, there is no room for error. That is how events become a part of history.

"Is there anyone who doubts that Alexander The Great ruled the earth, and died at the age of thirty three? It was a long time ago. Maybe he only ruled over one country and died at the age of sixty? Maybe he never existed at all? Maybe someone made up a fable to teach the virtue of ambition? Even though it happened so long ago, something that is so public and so well known gets written down in history and is carried forward to this day.

"David," I said, "We as a people should be especially sensitive to this subject. We don't have to go very far back in our history to find people denying events that we know happened. There are now books, articles, and entire web sites dedicated to proving that the Holocaust never occurred. They claim that it is all a plot of International Jewry to gather up world sympathy, so that the state of Israel should come into existence. How do we answer them? What is our response? And even if you tell me that they don't deserve an answer, because they postulate out of hatred and have no interest in truth, still what is our response to those who honestly want to know? How do we know that the Holocaust really happened?

"We have only one response: Listen. Listen as eye witness after eye witness tells their story. Listen to the accounts of entire towns being led out to dig their own graves. Listen to this man's retelling of what it was like in the crematorium at Treblinka. Listen as this woman describes what it was like to stand at the gas chambers of Auschwitz, and be forced to pry apart the dead bodies. Listen to the thousands of men, women and children, with numbers tattooed on their arms, telling you of their fate. And then ask yourself one question: What do you think? Is it possible for so many people, from so many different walks of life, from so many different cultures, and from so many different nationalities to gather together and perpetrate such a fraud? Would it work? Could it ever be pulled off?

"David, we don't believe the Holocaust happened—we know it. We know it because of the myriad people who were there, who survived, and now tell us what happened. We may not have been there, but we know with absolute knowledge what happened there.

"That is the same way that we know that the Torah came from God: because three million people couldn't lie. There is no possible way that such a remarkably public event could have been just fabricated and put on the record. There is no possible way that such an occurrence could be passed down generation to generation, talked about, studied, and discussed, if it were fictional.

"Even more, there is no way to falsify a belief that has been held as precious as life itself and as such was handed down from father to son, mother to daughter, generation to generation. Over the millennium, Jews have willingly given up their lives for their belief in God, and their belief in the revelation at Sinai. Sane, rational people from every walk of life and from every type of community were willing to lay down their lives for these convictions. When in the throes of death a mother turns to her child and says, *'My daughter, I may not know much, but this I know: there is a God in Heaven, who appeared to us on Sinai and gave us the Torah. I know this because my mother told me, and she knew it because her mother told her, and in turn her mother heard it from her mother, mother to daughter, mother to daughter all the way back in an unbroken chain.'*

"When a child hears this she knows that it's the truth. And, if it isn't one mother, but a nation of mothers and fathers, all telling the same story, all describing what their parents told them, who were in turn told by their parents, all the way back in time, then we know it is true.

"So, David and Susan, if you ask me, do I believe that the Torah was given by God to the Jewish people on Mt. Sinai? The answer is no, I don't believe it, I know it. Much like any fact in history isn't something that we believe in, but is something we know to be true. We know that the Magna Carta was the charter of English political and civil liberties, granted by King John at Runnymede in June 1215. That isn't something that we accept upon faith; it is something that we know to be true. So too we know that an event as public as God speaking to millions of people at the foot of Mt. Sinai is something that can't be falsified.

"When that event is then chronicled and recorded in exacting detail, and in that form passed down father to son, mother to daughter in an unbroken chain, spanning the generations; when this very same Torah is the heart blood of a people for over 3,000 years, and as such is studied, scrutinized, dissected and subjected to the most rigorous test of human understanding; when this is the one central truth that a nation takes with them from country to country, continent to continent, throughout a 2,000 year long exile—then it is not something that we believe in; it is something we know.

"Why don't we stop here.

"Susan," I said, "I don't know what your schedule looks like but you are more than welcome to join us next week."

"I'd love to," she replied.

Chapter 18: People Believe What They Want To Believe

"I had an interesting situation this week," David said, "and I thought that you would be the right person to discuss it with. We were having dinner one evening with a friend whom I haven't seen in quite some time, and the conversation turned to my increased awareness of religion. I told him that I was studying with a Rabbi, and we were getting into some of the fundamentals of man, and our purpose in this world, when he said to me, *'Do you really believe in God?'*

"I said, *'I sure do.'*

"He then said, *'I spent a lot of time thinking about this and he just didn't see how people could believe in God. How can you possibly believe in something that you can't see, something so remote, something that is so far removed from what we experience?'*

"The conversation turned when he said to me, *'If you really believe in God, prove to me that he exists.'* Rabbi, to be honest with you, I didn't succeed. It seemed that no matter what I said, he didn't accept my position. I have to admit that I left feeling frustrated."

I sat back in my chair for a moment, and then said, "David, a few years back I was teaching a class in the Synagogue. It was during one of our weekly sessions in Bible study, when a bright young man, who was then in dental school, made a comment that stuck with me. He said, *'All of the miracles that we have been studying are very impressive—the Ancient Egyptians being smitten with the plagues, then the splitting of the sea. It's all great but it happened so long ago. I don't need all of that to happen, if God would show me just one miracle then I would believe.'*

"I thought about his remark for some time till I came to the realization that he had stumbled upon one of the very basic tenets of our belief system.

"I asked my young friend if he thought that miracles make a person believe in God. He answered, *'Of course, anyone would believe if they had seen the type of miracles described in the Bible.'*

"I said to him, *'I have one simple question. Why didn't the Ancient Egyptians believe in God?'*

'What do you mean? They were wicked; they were the ones who wanted to kill the Jews,' he answered.

'I understand, but they experienced the very same miracles that the Jewish nation did. They lived through the entire ten plagues. They saw the same manifestation of God's hand, as the Jews did, yet the vast majority of them never came to any recognition of the dominion of God. Quite the opposite, till the bitter end most of them denied God. According to your thesis that miracles make a person believe in God, how could that be? How could a nation live through such obvious and clear miracles and not believe?'

"David, to put this question into better focus, let's imagine what is was like to be an Egyptian living at that time. Let's picture Anwar, a simple, reasonably honest, hard working land owner, standing in the hot sun wondering how he is going to get his cows to market. Along comes his friend Nachmad.

'Hey Anwar, did you hear what's going on?' Nachmad asks.

'No what?'

'Well, this tall, majestic Hebrew named Moses comes walking into the palace with his brother Aaron, and starts threatening King Pharaoh.'

'Hey, that's not too bright,' Anwar responds. 'Remember what happened to the last guy who tried that? Pharaoh's wife is now using his dried bones for clothing pins.'

'Yeah, but anyway, he says that God sent him to tell Pharaoh to let the Jewish people go.'

'Which God sent him?'

'No, not one of our Gods, Moses is talking about this super God, who, he says, created the heavens and earth and runs everything.'

'Oh come now, Nachmad, everyone thinks that their God is the best.'

'No, no, you don't understand, he started doing all of these bizarre things. First he threw his staff down on the ground, and it turned into a snake. Then he put his hand in his shirt, and it came out white with leprosy. Then finally, he threw water on the ground, and it turned into blood. And here's the kicker, he threatened that if Pharaoh doesn't let the Jewish people go, this God of his is going to turn all of the water in all of Egypt into blood.'

'Oh, come now, Nachmad, do you really believe that?'

'Well, I may or may not, but I'll tell you this much, Pharaoh sure took him seriously.'

"Now Anwar worshiped his fair share of idols in his day—not really sure if he believes in any of them—but why take chances? So he makes sure to hide away a couple of extra barrels of water, just in case.

"Then, on the appointed day at the appointed time, lo and behold, all of the water in all of Egypt turns into blood. Not just the water in the Nile; the water in the sinks, water in the bathtubs, water in the barrels, water in the fields, all of the water anywhere to be found turns into blood. If the Egyptians had water stored in the basement, it turned to blood. If they stored some in a jug in the attic, it turned to blood. If they bit into a fruit, instead of juice they got a spurt of blood.

"Let's keep in mind that blood isn't just red, colored water; it is thick and it smells. Wherever there had been water, it was now blood—except for water owned by the Jews. If a Jewish person was drinking water, it remained water.

"Now, let us imagine that our friend Anwar has a few Jewish slaves, one of whom is working in the fields that day. While watching all of this, Anwar says to himself, *'I may not be the sharpest triangle in the pyramid ,but even I can figure out that something is going on here.'* He calls over his Jewish slave who is happily drinking a glass of cool fresh water.

'Hey, Isaac, come here.'

'Yes, Master.'

'What is that you are drinking?'

'It's water, Sir.'

'Yeah, I know that. Now wipe that smirk off your face and give me some of that.'

"So the Jewish slave hands the cup of water over, and as the cup passes from his hand to the hand of his Egyptian master, it turns from water into blood.

'Hey, take that back!' Anwar screams.

"As Isaac takes back the cup it turns back from blood into water.

"Anwar says, *'Now give me that!'*

"Again, as soon as the cup leaves Isaac's hand, the water turns back to blood. This goes on, back and forth, water to blood, blood to water, water to blood.

"Finally Anwar thinks for a moment and says:

'Now, listen here, you and I are going to drink at the same time. As I put my lips to the cup, you are going to do the same thing. And remember, no tricks or I will whip you, understand?!'

They both stand there lips pressed against the cup.

'Ready. One, two, three... Ughhhhhh!' Anwar shrieks, spitting out blood, while our friend Isaac is drinking clear fresh water.

"Now, David, that is a very impressive feat. It isn't everyday that all of the water in all of Egypt turns into blood. The concept that every person living in Egypt saw clearly and directly was, that God is the one Who controls nature. How does liquid change from one state to another, depending upon who is holding it? The message God was delivering was as clear as day; blood is red and thick because God so decrees it should be. The minute God decrees that it should be otherwise, it changes to clear drinking water. There is no such thing as the laws of nature existing independently of God, rather those are the rules and guidelines that God uses to run this world. But the moment that He sees fit to change them, it is as if they never were.

"This wasn't some theoretical concept that the Egyptians were exposed to. This was something that every Egyptian man, woman, and child saw in front of their eyes. There was no room for doubt because of the clarity with which they saw this. They lived through an undeniable demonstration of God's control over every facet of nature. They saw that God was there in their everyday life. Not a million miles away up in Heaven, but right there. Yet they didn't come to belief.

"What is even more astounding is that God could have taken the Jewish nation out of Egypt in any manner which He chose. The reason He chose to do it that way was to make it clear for all to see that God is present in the world, so that anyone witnessing these events would come to the inescapable conclusion: there is a God in the world who controls and runs the world. This was to be one time in history that God would show his dominion over nature, so that all future generations should be able to point back at that moment, as a basis for their belief.

"Yet the amazing fact was the Egyptians did not come to that belief! They lived through all of the miracles of plagues, seeing God right there, and still they didn't reach the most compelling and obvious conclusion: this is the hand of God. Until the bitter end, almost all of the Egyptians denied that they were witnessing the hand of God.

"We have to ask ourselves how that could be. How could intelligent, reasonable people see such clear manifestations of God's hand, and not believe?

"If we spend a little time reviewing some of the events that transpired, I think that we will find this question even more perplexing.

"The Bible is very clear, that before each plague, Moses came to Pharaoh's palace and warned him exactly what was going to happen. Each time that Moses gave a warning, not only did the plague happen, but it happened exactly as he said it would, when he said it would.

"Egypt was the most powerful nation at that time; it was also by far the wealthiest. As an agricultural society, their wealth was held in their fields and flocks. During the next ten months they suffered ruinous disaster. Piece by piece, their resources and all that they had built up were destroyed. All of their fields were wiped out, and all of their livestock killed. Each plague was specifically designed to show that nature is directly controlled by God. Each plague showed another dimension of God's control over the world.

"By the last plague, Moses had a captive audience. The Egyptians had now lived through ten months of warnings and plagues, they found that every time Moses promised something would happen, it did, exactly as he had predicted, down to the minutest detail. At this point there were many who did believe in God. A group of 'first born' came to Pharaoh's palace and offered an ultimatum to the king: either let the Jews go, or we will dethrone you. Not only did Pharaoh not listen, he had the entire group killed to subdue the uprising.

"Then, on the appointed time in the appointed manner, every first born in Egypt died.

"It didn't matter if the oldest born child was five or fifty five, he died. It didn't matter if there was one son or ten, only the oldest died. If in one house there were six boys ranging from sixteen to twenty six and the next to oldest was taller, stronger and looked five years older then his oldest brother, the one born first died.

"But it wasn't only the first born; the verse in the Bible says that there wasn't a house that didn't have a death. The Talmud tells us, if there was a first born male child in the home he died, if not, then the oldest male in the house died. So if a particular home had only girls, then the father died.

"Who was keeping track of which son was oldest? Who recorded which newborn came out first? It was clear to everyone living in Egypt then, that God watches over everything, records all, and nothing escapes His notice.

"What is even more moving is that in many houses there was more than one death. The commentaries explain to us that the Egyptian women were promiscuous. So you might have a house where a woman had a number of affairs over the years, and bore children from other men, then each child that was the first born of a particular man, died.

"Let's imagine this for a moment: a woman, we'll call her Cleopatra, had five boys, and all of them die in this plague. As it turns out, thirty years before she had an affair, became pregnant, and had a child from that union, her first born.

Five years later she had an affair with another man, and had a child through that union, her second son, the first for that fellow. Five years later the same story with a third fellow, and five years after that again with another individual; until she ended up having five sons, each a 'first born', of different fathers.

"Could we imagine what it must have been like for this woman, as she buried five of her sons on the same day? What did she say to herself?

'Thirty years ago I had an affair with a guy. No one anywhere knew about it! It was the best kept secret, we made up to meet in a field five miles away from civilization. There wasn't a soul in the world who knew about it! Now that son is dead. Five years after that I had an affair with a different man, we met somewhere out in an inn so far from anyone. We were so careful, my husband never found out, not even my best friend knew, and for 25 years now I've been keeping this secret! Now that son is dead. Five years after that I met a man on a back road, we went into the woods, it was a one time thing, there wasn't a human being in the world who could have possibly known about it! Now that son is dead! What does this mean? What is happening? How could this possibly be?'

"What this woman saw with absolute clarity was that God was watching. That God is ever present and watches every event that transpires on the face of this planet. This woman got to see clearly that everything is recorded, weighed and measured. Very few accounts are settled immediately, but in the end absolute justice is meted out. Often times it won't be until years later, maybe not even in a person's lifetime, but in the end someone is watching and keeping track.

"The amazing part of all of this is that she didn't learn this through some theoretical lecture about morality and God. She didn't hear a course in highfalutin philosophy that has little bearing on her life. She saw it and felt it with exacting, painful clarity. It happened to her and it was real.

"Could we imagine how strongly this woman now understood the control and sovereignty that God maintains over the world?!

"Let's take this a step further. Let's imagine that we get to walk with our friend Cleopatra to the cemetery as she buries her five sons. We overhear her talking to some of the women:

'You know, girls, this just strengthens what I have always said to you, we must be so careful about our health, watch our cholesterol, get yearly check ups, and exercise regularly. Why, just look what happened to my five sons. Please, girls, promise me, no more red meat!'

"Would we have words to describe our amazement over the rank of stupidity of such a statement? Is it possible to even imagine that a human being, someone who looks, speaks, and thinks, like you or I, could ever say such words?

In reality, that is the equivalent of what the Egyptians did. Even after the final and worst plague, did they now believe? Did they now throw in the towel? Did they say, we were wrong and now repent? No! Not only did they not admit they had been wrong, but they actually chased down the Jewish nation and followed them into the sea! Is there a way to make some sense out of such unintelligent behavior? To watch a sophisticated nation go to their death without even awakening to the realization that maybe, just maybe, there is a God in this world, and He is orchestrating these events.

"You see, David, these people were exercising their Free Will to believe or not. We, humans, have this fantastic ability to believe what we want, irrespective of logic or truth. If a person doesn't want to believe, you can show them irrefutable evidence, and they just won't accept it. We have this uncanny ability not be moved by truth and logic, but by emotions and desires. As part of the Master Plan for creation, God gave us this ability to believe what we want to believe.

"As a Religious person, this is something that I experience on a daily basis. I look at a world that is so vast, so diverse, and yet so harmonious in all of its complexity. From the cosmic dimension of 100's upon 100's of billions of stars, all moving in controlled orbits, down to the subatomic level, all components meshing in such mind numbing symmetry and accord—all screaming out the undeniable fact: there is a Creator and Master to this world. Yet we find rational, intelligent people saying things like, *'it just happened,' 'by luck, by chance,' 'all of the wisdom of the universe just is...'*

"I remember when my wife was pregnant with our fourth child, the other children were already in school, and it became a family project to calculate the development of the unborn fetus. Looking at pictures of embryos at different stages of development, we would imagine what stage our unborn family member was up to. It was a moving experience to watch the steps of a human baby forming; we saw such wisdom in it all. From the beginning of the nubs that are to become the limbs, to the forming of the spinal cortex, the entire development of a vastly complex organism is so controlled, so orchestrated. The most sophisticated explosion of life, all happening far away from the human eye. To my family and to me personally it was a very moving religious experience.

"As it would happen, our baby was born on Yom Kippur. You had to see me, a young Rabbi, dressed in my holiday finest, frantically rushing my wife to the hospital. David, as I stood there in the delivery room, I felt a rush of emotion, experiencing this miracle called birth; the most magnificent, stupendous occurrence, the bringing forth of life, happening on our most Holy day. I felt as high as a kite.

"Thank God, everything went well, the baby came out a healthy, fully formed, beautiful baby girl. I was so appreciative for this gift of life that I wanted to sing out Psalms of Thanksgiving. At that moment when my mind was fully enveloped in appreciation to God for what He gave us, I said to the nurse, something like, *'Wow, what a miracle!' To which she answered, 'Yes isn't it wonderful, how nature has evolved.'*

"Now, that wasn't the time for a philosophical debate, so I didn't comment. But it brought home this point more clearly than ever. Here was a woman, who on a daily basis was involved in one of the most miraculous parts of Creation; she participated and helped in the bringing forth of life. Is there anyone who could deny the holiness of such an act? Is there anyone who isn't awed by the magnificence of a fully formed human baby arising from a tiny seed and egg, once invisible to the naked eye? All of the wisdom of the human body encoded in the subatomic DNA, a micro-computer, housed in each cell, controlling the formation of millions upon millions of cells; some becoming part of the bone structure, some becoming part of the organ systems, and others becoming the gray matter that makes up the human brain. Do we have words to describe the wonder of it all? Not only didn't she see anything special about it, to her it was just another cog in the evolutionary process.

"In Jewish thought one of the recommended methods of learning to see God is to look out at the world. When a person sees the beauty of this universe, the conformity of every part working together as a unit, everything so orderly, so reliable: the sun rising every morning exactly at the appointed time; the tides always pulling in the pre-described manner; the forces of nature all so seemingly untamed, tempests out of control, yet always performing within a predictable, set pattern. The ocean never exceeding its bounds, the moon always appearing on time, the antelope always mating in season, and producing offspring to carry on after them—all diverse parts conforming to a master plan, so that the world itself cries out: there is a master to this house.

"Yet we see over and over again, that while there is great debate amongst the scientific community, there remains a core of individuals who affirm, that there is no Creator, the world evolved by chance, by random luck; it was nothing but a roll of the cosmic dice.

"David, I don't want to get into an entire discussion about evolution right now, maybe at some future time we can. One point I do want to bring home is that if the greatest supernatural miracles ever shown to man, couldn't convince an Egyptian society that there is a God, Who created the world, it shouldn't surprise us to find intelligent, well read people in our midst who can look at the miracle of creation and deny God. The reason has to do with the very nature of the human fabric.

"Do you remember the old TV show Star Trek? One of the most memorable characters was Mr. Spock. He was the fellow with the pointy ears, the Vulcan. While everyone else on the starship Enterprise was subject to human emotions, he came from a different planet and was only capable of thinking logically. In fact he couldn't understand emotions. We, humans, tend to think of ourselves as Mr. Spock. We assume that our approach to life situations is totally logical, totally thought out. We work with this unspoken assumption that our emotions are the way that we feel, but we don't allow them to alter the way we view major issues. Unfortunately, we couldn't be further from the truth.

"As much as we hate to admit it to ourselves, most of our real decisions and choices are made emotionally. To show you what I mean, have you seen the latest Marlboro Billboards? All that appears is an oversized picture of the Marlboro man, not even a mention of the cigarette brand, just a close-up of the Marlboro man, skin as thick as leather, his face so tight that it would crack if he smiled. The focus of it all: the white cancer stick dangling out of his lips. David, did you ever wonder why they do that? Why don't they just make a whole bunch of logical statements, like: *'Our cigarettes are the best?' 'For the finest flavor and taste, eight out of ten smokers prefer our brand of cigarettes to any other.'* Wouldn't that be the logical way of selling cigarettes?

"The truth is that it would. That would be the logical way to sell, but advertisers know full well that logic doesn't sell anything. Because consumers don't buy based on logic, they buy based on emotions. The implication in the Marlboro® commercial is clear: if you want to be cool like the Marlboro® Man, you'll need to smoke Marlboro. You see, David, they really aren't selling their brand of cigarettes, they are selling something much more in demand, something much more basic to the human wants and desires. They are selling prestige. Be Cool, smoke Marlboro®.

"Now, you may ask me, does that really work? Is anyone really gullible enough to fall for that? After all, I go to work everyday in a suit, I don't ride a horse. I don't wear stirrups, and even the good ole cowboys drive jeeps these days, they're just faster, and easier to keep. So is anyone going to say, *'Boy, I want to be just like the Marlboro® man sitting up there so strong and handsome, with skin as hard as leather, so I better run down to the store and get myself a pack right now.'* Who in their right mind is going to say that?

"The answer is, no one in their right mind. But it doesn't matter, because Madison Avenue knows that no one makes decisions in their right mind. Most of our decisions as consumers are made in our deeply recessed subconscious; the part of us that wants things, the part of us that craves things. When I decide to buy this model car or that one, rarely does it have to do with performance and function; it has to do with perceptions and feelings. Is this <u>my kind</u> of car? What does that model mean to me? How will I feel when I drive around in it? How does driving this kind of car position me among my friends and neighbors? That decision touches upon a part of me that is deeply recessed, my emotional makeup—and that part isn't limited to the rules of logic and sensibility. Granted I may rationalize my decision, I may come up with very solid arguments to support my choice, but if I was brutally honest with myself, I would soon see that most of my decisions are made based on how I feel about the item, the rational arguments are brought in after the fact to defend my choice to my logical thinking side.

"Our emotions affect us more than we'd care to admit. They affect our decisions in what we buy, they influence our opinion as to what we like, and the way we feel about things. They can even go so far as to effect what we believe in.

"To illustrate this point, Rabbi Elchonon Wassermann, one of Judaism's great leaders of the early 20th century asks a powerful philosophical question. He says: the Bible gives us a specific commandment—to believe in God. How is such a commandment possible, he asks? If I already believe in God, then I don't need a commandment to believe, I already do. If I don't believe in God, how will a commandment help? I don't believe. The Bible can command me to do something physical, to give charity, or to help a widow. I may not wish to, I might not be in the mood, but if there is a direct command, hopefully, I will do it anyway. Here we are dealing with something that is so elusive, something that is inside my heart. If my heart doesn't believe, what shall I say? *'Heart, believe. I command you to believe!'* It just doesn't work. If, in fact, I don't believe in God, how are all of the commandments in the world going to help?

"His answer is as profound as it is simple. He says, that in truth the Bible isn't commanding a person to believe in God, per se. Rather the commandment is: Be honest. Be open. Look at the world, see its beauty, its diversity, its complexity, and ask yourself **honestly**, what do you think? Do you think that it just happened? Do you think it just occurred?

"So often our agendas get in the way of our thinking. If we accept God, then it means that we have been wrong up until now, and that runs against our whole mode of thinking. If we accept God, then there are going to be certain requirements, things that we may have to do, or things that we will not be able to do. Therefore, it is just so much easier, so much more convenient if there is no God. There are many reasons why a person won't want to accept what their mind tells them is true.

"The Bible is saying one thing, put away those agendas. Forget the consequences. I don't care if you change your lifestyle an iota or not. Just tell me one thing, what do you honestly think? Look at the world and tell me, did it just happen? Did all of the extraordinary components of this world just occur? Could all of this intricate complexity, each system so dependent on the next, just come about, without a higher wisdom guiding it all? If a person does this exercise, and is able to put away all other issues and focus on this one question: is there a Creator of this world?—then logic will bring them to see the hand of God.

"You see, David," I concluded, "I don't think that we are accustomed to thinking honestly. We have our preconceived notions, our own world view, and everything that we come across gets filtered through those preset assumptions. If we find input that supports our positions we latch on to it. If we find conclusions that we are uncomfortable with, no matter how logically compelling they may be, we find reasons to reject them. Our wants and desires color everything we see and distorts our vision. What the Bible is telling us is to put away all of our pre-established notions, and just approach this from an intellectual vantage point: what do you honestly think?

"If you have a discussion with someone, and they say, *'Prove that God exists,'* their real intention will determine whether you will be successful. If what they mean is, *'I am open. I have questions and honestly want to hear the answers,'* then it is a simple matter to show such a person the hand of God in our infinitely complex and integrated world. Can such a fantastic work just come into being on its own? Doesn't the house scream out to its Creator?

"But, if they are really saying, *'I don't want to believe in God. I find it too hard to change my perspective on life, and I don't want to hear what you are saying,'* then there is no way under this sun that you can convince them. The most logically compelling arguments and the most irrefutable facts won't move them. What they are really saying is, *'my mind has been made up; I already know the correct answer.'* If, in fact, we were Mr. Spock, and our actions, thoughts and decisions were based on logic, then it would be an easy enough task to convince such a person. The reality is that we humans just don't function that way. So short of handcuffing his mind to a position that he refuses to hear, there is no way to prove that God exists, or, for that matter, any other position that he doesn't want to hear.

"That is why the Ancient Egyptians didn't believe in God. Despite having seen miracles that were so clear and obvious. Despite having seen the hand of God. Despite seeing miracles that were so undeniable, that they are the underpinning of our faith, now thousands of years later. They saw and didn't believe, because God created us with this fantastic ability to believe what we want to believe. That is why even if we were to witness miracles today, if we were predisposed against believing in God, we wouldn't necessarily change our position. It all stems from this one phenomenon, people don't believe what is honest or truthful. People don't even believe what is logical or reasonable. **People believe what they want to believe."**

"Rabbi," Susan said, "what you are proposing is that the average man can lie to himself. He can live in a world of delusion, just inventing things to suit his interests and somehow fooling himself into believing them."

"Exactly."

"Rabbi, I don't see things that way. Maybe my professional training is influencing me, but I work with the assumption that if something is true, any human would have to admit to it—if the facts were presented to them in a logical, well documented fashion. How can a person who is wise, clear headed and insightful believe things that he knows aren't true, just because he wants to?"

Chapter 19: I Never Do Anything Wrong

"Susan," I said, "I am afraid this type of phenomena is far more common than we like to admit. Let me show you an interesting example. In the 1930s, there lived one of the most notorious gangsters who ever shot up the streets of New York City, he was called Two Gun Crowley. He was also known as Crowley, the cop killer. The Police Commissioner at the time, described him as one of the most ruthless, hardened killers, who ever walked the streets of New York. He would kill at the drop of a feather.

"Two Gun fired his last bullet in a shoot-out with police in an apartment on West End Avenue. Surrounded by 150 policemen, who used everything from tear gas, to machine guns mounted on surrounding rooftops, he still managed to hold them at bay for over an hour. Ten thousand onlookers watched, as the streets of Manhattan sounded with the explosion of machine gun fire. Finally, after being shot in the chest, the wrote his last message, a note drenched in his blood, which read:

To whom it may concern:

Under my coat lies a lonely heart, but a kind heart, a heart that would do no man harm.'

"And he signed it!

"Only hours before he was in the park, sitting in a car with his girlfriend. A police officer passing by asked him for his license and registration, at which point Two Gun reached into his coat, pulled out a revolver, and shot the cop dead. He then jumped out of the car, pulled out the officer's service revolver, added another bullet for good measure, and then drove off. He could have just as easily have driven off without shooting the officer, but why take any chances. *'A kind heart, one that would do no man harm.'*

"Our story doesn't end here. Two Gun Crowley managed to live through the shoot-out. The police broke in, arrested him, and he stood trial. He was sentenced to death. On his way to the electric chair, he was overheard saying, *'This is what I get for defending myself.'*

"What makes this story significant for us is that I don't think that Two Gun Crowley was insane, or that his self perception was so off that he was demented. His behavior seems to be quite common for the criminal element. In one of his books Dale Carnegie writes, that he had an ongoing correspondence with the warden of Sing Sing prison, who explained to him that not one of his inmates thought he was guilty. Every one of them had some reason why they had to be quick on the trigger, or why they had to live a life of crime. I think it is true across every station in life. No one thinks of themselves as bad, or evil, or even that they do things that are wrong.

"When I was on staff at our local Jewish high school, one of the students was caught stealing. These were all fine boys, from the best of homes, so I was quite surprised to hear that one of them would be preying on his own classmates and friends. As it turned out, I knew the young man quite well, I had been counseling him for some time, and we were very friendly. He was a lovely, respectful, well liked fellow who was quite popular in his class. I was perplexed. I couldn't understand how he could bring himself to steal from his friends. I sat him down to talk about the incident, and in the course of conversation it came out. Without a touch of remorse, he said to me, *'Rabbi, you have to understand, everybody needs money. Some guys get money from their parents, other guys have jobs. This is how I make money.'*

"What amazed me was that to him it wasn't a crime. In his mind it wasn't stealing—this was the *'way he made money.'*

"It seems that this type of thought process is common among thieves. The mental viewpoint of most criminals is: *'Everyone would steal. The only reason that other people don't steal is because they aren't as bright as I am—they just aren't as bold. But believe me, if they were as sharp as me, they would be out there stealing all day long.'*

"Susan," I said. "This phenomenon is an essential component in man. We may call this rationalizing, we may call this a defense mechanism, but there is a fundamental reason why we human beings do this, why we have to do this. It has to do with our very nature.

"Do you remember we spoke about the two parts of man's soul: his Animal Soul and his Spiritual Soul? His Animal Soul contains all of the basic desires necessary to keep the human species in existence. The Spiritual Soul functions in a completely different realm. That part of man, the pure Godlike part, is so perfect that it can do no wrong. By its very nature it can only serve others and be generous. That part was preprogrammed for perfection. If man was created only with these two competing parts man would do 'good', in fact he would do only 'good'—but not because he <u>chose</u> to, but because he had to, because that would be his very nature.

"When God put man on this planet, it was with a very specific task: to allow man to grow. To give man the opportunity to perfect himself by fighting the battles of life, by actively choosing correctly, thereby shaping himself into what he will be for eternity. By definition that means there has to be a challenge, there has to be a real reason to want to go against his better nature. For man to be responsible for creating the person he becomes, it has to be something that he did, something that he consciously chose, not something that he was preconditioned to do. For that to happen man has to be able to choose good or evil, with both sides being equal to him; his will alone determining which he chooses. So, to allow for Free Will, there was another component that needed to be added to man."

"I don't understand," Susan asked, "what would be lacking in terms of Free will? As you said, God implanted in the human an Animal Soul, with hungers, appetites, and self serving desires—so now man wants things, he desires things. He now has challenges and decisions to make. With a Spiritual Soul that tells him what is right, and desires that run counter to his understanding, he is perfectly poised for the shaping of his very nature. So what more do we need for man to have Free Will?"

"Susan," I said, "Do you have Free Will to put your hand in a fire?"

"Do I have Free Will?"

"Yes," I said. "Let's say, I offer you a hundred dollars to put your hand in a fire, do you have Free Will to do it?"

"Well, I guess I do," Susan answered. "I sure don't think that I would do it, though."

"I think what you just said is very accurate; you have Free Will, but you wouldn't do it, because it is a stupid, self-destructive thing for you to do, and so, you wouldn't do it. When we talk about Free Will, we don't mean the theoretical ability to do something. We mean there has to be a real challenge, a real fight. Both sides have to be appealing, both choices have to have merit, and the human must be able to go either way.

"The problem is that if man was created with these two parts only, there would be no Free Will, because the Spiritual Soul of man is so pure, it simply won't let him do something wrong. It would never allow him to do something selfish, cruel, or mean. It would rebel and scream out: *'How could you do that? That's nasty. You are hurting another human being! What right do you have to put your self interests in front of another person's?'* Granted he would have the physical ability to do things that were wrong. But he wouldn't do them; much like you wouldn't put your hand in a fire.

"Therein lies one of the greatest dilemmas in creation: how do you take this pinnacle of greatness, man, who has a soul that is considered holier than an angel, and counter-balance this loftiness? If the goal in creation is to have a level playing field, where man can truly exercise his Free Will, how do you balance out against the majestic soul of man?

"To solve this perplexing dilemma, God in his infinite wisdom gave man just such a balancing agent: **Imagination.**

"When God created man, not only did He implant the two aspects of a Spiritual Soul and an Animal Soul, He introduced this third component of Imagination to interplay between the two. This quality of imagination serves as an equilibrium between our logical thought process and our emotions. Now, when man approaches an issue, he isn't only limited to pure thought. Now, the very way that he looks at things is subjective.

"If I want something, if I desire it, my emotions can affect my entire way of understanding that issue. No longer is it something that I know is wrong but want to do anyway. I now have this ability to create—almost by instinct—entire rationales and theologies that change my view. My emotions color my opinions and thought process, and affect the very way that I view life. Now my sense of morality is no longer set in concrete but can change at will, because I no longer think only with my logical side, I also have this component of creative imagination that mixes into my very thought process. Now man can, in fact, do exactly as he wants. If he wishes to chose selfish interests, his Spiritual Soul can't stop him, because in his convoluted sense, what he does, whatever he does, is right. So when that Voice Inside screams out *'Do something meaningful with your life.' Now there is an answer: 'I am doing something. I am doing something noble, proper, and right. And it is so, because I will it to be!'*

"Now, finally, I am Free. Free from the shackles of having to do what is right because that higher side of me demands it from me; free to chart my course in life exactly as I see fit. If my agenda is self-serving aggrandizement, within arms reach I can create an entire thought process that not only justifies this, but uplifts it to a grand thing. I am no longer restricted to doing only what my Spiritual Soul tells me is right. I have the ability to change what is right and what is wrong.

"Now, I am no longer restricted by the rules of logic as guided by absolute truth, I can shape that logic. I can rationalize and create entire philosophies that, at least on a certain level, I believe. Since I make the rules of what is right and what is wrong, no one, not even my Voice Inside can lecture me. Now I'm free to chose my course in life, because not only do I have Free Choice in how I act—I now have Free Choice in what I believe—*I can believe what I want to believe.*

"This is something that happens all the time. We may not focus on it, but we have this inborn capacity to believe things that we know aren't true. Think of the last time you were watching a movie and the hero was walking down a deserted alleyway. The tempo of the music quickens. The alleyway gets darker. The shadows play against the cold brick wall. You sense the danger. You feel the impending doom. Then it happens. Three guys jump out. Our hero gets hit, he falls to the ground. One guy hits him, another jumps on his back. He rolls. He punches. The first thug crumples up in pain. Punch! Kick! Punch! Kick! The third thug jumps into the fight. Your pulse quickens and you feel your heart pounding. *'Come on hit him! Duck. Now kick him!'* You want to scream.

"If you were to stop now and take your pulse, it would be racing, and your hands would be cold and sweaty. Now ask yourself one very simple question. What is going on here? This is a movie. Those are paid actors up there on the screen. You know that. You know they aren't really hitting each other. It's made up. It's pretend. So why are you sweating? Even more, let's say it was real. Let's say there was a real honest to goodness fight going on, and the Hero of our story was being beaten up. Still why are you sweating? Why is your heart pounding? That's him up there getting beat up—not you.

"But, it is you. As any casting director knows, the secret to good acting is how much the audience identifies with the actor. Meaning how much they see themselves in that role. So that it isn't our hero who is walking down that alleyway—it is you. It isn't our hero who is getting jumped—it is *you*. When you watch good acting you find yourself involved, intimately involved, as if it were happening to you. Have you ever cried during a movie? Have you ever fallen in love? You didn't feel

those emotions because something good happened to that actor. It was because it happened to you. You were there. You were in that story. It was you who just discovered her long lost brother. It was you who was languishing in prison, and it was you who made that come back from cancer and went on to compete in the Olympics.

"This ability to fantasize, to take something that is pure fiction and see it as if it were real, is something that God implanted in us, for a specific purpose; it allows us to see things as we wish them to be. With this capacity of imagination, we can believe things—things that may not be true, things that we know aren't true. We are able to accept them as true. We have this ability to see what we want to see as if it was real, and because of this we can believe what we want to believe.

"This phenomena plays out in our life, when we find ourselves face to face with something that we want to do, but know is wrong. This creative process begins—this process of inventing entire philosophies and theologies and then believing in them. I imagine my young friend, the high school student, went through something like this when he would see another fellow's money. He wanted the money, and yet knew that he couldn't take it. So now what? Take it? That's stealing, that's wrong. I can't do that. Not take it? I want it. So the battle begins; two voices, each one presenting its side.

'Come on, why don't you take that money, you could really use it, couldn't you?'

'What are you, crazy, that is stealing, I can't do that.'

'Come on, don't be such a holy roller, everybody has some fault, so this is yours, what is so bad about one little fault, we're all human, you know, come on now, take it.'

'I will not! That's not the kind of person I am. I don't do those kinds of things.'

'Look, other fellows have money. Some guys have jobs, some guys get money from their parents. Everyone has money, except you. Don't you deserve to have things as well? Who takes care of you? No one. That's who! You're all alone in this world, and if you don't take care of yourself no one will. You don't have it easy, you know. Come on now, take it, take the money, just do it.'

'You're crazy, I can't take it, it belongs to Sam, Sam is my friend, I can't steal from Sam.'

'What did Sam ever do for you? Besides, is he better than you? Did he do anything to deserve more than you? Why should he have things that you don't have? I happen to think that it's plain unfair for Sam to have more then you. Not only that, I think it's wrong. It's wrong for Sam to have more than you! The really proper thing would be for Sam to share with you. Since he hasn't offered, the only right thing is to help Sam do what he should have done on his own. So I want you to go right now and help Sam do the right thing. Go take it, it's a Mitzvah!'

"Susan," I said, "this would seem comical if it didn't really happen. If this wasn't what actually goes on in our mind, we could find it quite humorous. It's not funny, because it is us. We do things just like this, all the time. We may not focus on it, we may not even be aware of the process, but function it does. The human comes up with the most fanciful, creative rationales, not only to justify what he does, but to make it the right thing to do.

"Rabbi Israel Salanter once said: 'The Talmud tells us, if a person sins once, he perceives his action as a sin. If he repeats that sin, it now changes from a sin to something permitted'. The act is no longer in the category of something that he shouldn't do; it is now a permitted action.' Rabbi Salanter continues, 'What happens if he repeats that sin a third time? Then in his mind the action becomes a Mitzvah, a positive commandment, something he should do.'

"As I get on in life, I see this over and over again. No one does anything wrong! There is always a reason, a rational, an answer. *"This situation is different. The normal rules don't apply to me. What more could be expected out of me? Anyone who was in my place would have done the same."* We humans have this uncanny ability to create entire world views, sometimes very whimsical ones, to justify what we have done. Rare is the man, who can look you in the eye, and say, I have done wrong. Most often what we hear are stories, stories that start with excuses and end with justifications, but always consistent with one theme: I wasn't wrong. I was justified and correct in what I did. Even if we get that rare 'I was wrong,' very soon thereafter comes that ever present caveat, *but...*

"This situation would be interesting enough if we only did this to others, but we do it all the time—to ourselves. We create these illusions, entire fantasies that justify our behavior to ourselves. Why can't I just say the words, *'This is wrong? I know I shouldn't do it, but I want to do it anyway.'* Those words seem never, ever, ever, to come out of my mouth. It seems as if my teeth would chatter, my skull would shake, and my entire existence would be in jeopardy, if I had to make that admission.

"Why? What is that so hard? Why can't I just say, *'This is wrong? It isn't proper, I know I shouldn't do it, but I want to do it, and I am going to do it anyway?'* Psychologists will use words like *defense mechanisms*, and *self-protection*, but this isn't defending me against someone else, this is what is going on inside my mind, and no one else is listening. This is a conversation between me and me; so what is the problem?

"The answer is that I have to rationalize my behavior to myself, because that part of me, my Spiritual Soul wouldn't stand for me to do anything wrong—it wouldn't allow it. It's that simple, I can't do something that is wrong. So there is only one choice if I want to do it—I must make it right. I must invent a theory or a way of viewing things that turns something that is wrong, clearly wrong, into something that is okay. *'Listen, other people do it.' 'It can't be that bad.' 'Plenty of people do far worse things.'* If this activity is something that I do regularly then it isn't enough for it to be okay, it has to become a good thing to do. I will create an entire thought process to explain, why this is not something wrong, this is really a positive act, and a service to mankind. A little mental sleight of hand, and now everything is permitted, everything is okay.

"Ridiculous? Yes. Ludicrous? Most certainly, but that is us. That is the human condition, and it is time that we woke up to it. We never do anything wrong. Period! No matter what.

"Don't misunderstand me, we can make mistakes. Anyone can do that. We can even make mistakes in judgment, that is excusable. I am speaking about things that are intrinsically wrong; things that if I did, I would be guilty of being inconsiderate, or rude, or of putting my interests in front of someone else's. It's those types of things that you will never, ever find me doing. No matter how glaring, no matter how obvious it is to everyone else, in my mind it was 'justified and deserved.'

"The most heinous villains all had a self-redeeming philosophy. They had a view point, a way of looking at things that not only justified what they did, it made it a good thing. Hitler didn't say something like, *'It is wrong to kill innocent men, women, and children, but I hate them, so let's do it anyway.' He wrote an 800 page treatise, Mein Kamph,* where he outlined the world's problems, particularly the problems of Germany, and how the Jews were the cause of it all. In his rhetoric it is a good deed to kill a Jew. *'Much like when one kills a mosquito, one doesn't feel remorse; it serves very little purpose in this world, it is a nuisance. So too when one kills a Jew he should have the same attitude. He should understand that he is helping rid Germany and the world of a plague, the poisoner of all people, International Jewry.'*

"Do you remember the defense that almost every Nazi hid behind at the Nuremberg Trials: *'I was only following orders?'* Susan, I think there is some truth to that.

"I don't for a minute question the horrific nature of the Nazi beasts, and I don't have an ounce of forgiveness in my blood for what they perpetrated against our people. Still, I believe that many of them were doing just that, *'only following orders.'* I doubt there were many Nazis who were strong enough to justify to themselves the murder of innocent women and children. They were human and even in them there was a Voice Inside that screamed out:

'Hanz, how can you do this? These are people, human beings just like you. They have done nothing wrong. How can you do this?'

"There has to be some answer to that voice. A human being can't ignore that voice, he has to respond.

"So, the truly wicked, powerfully evil members of the Nazi party shouted those lines to themselves, and believed them:

'The Jews are vermin, all that is bad in Germany, is because of the Jews. It is either the Jews or the fatherland, and I choose Germany. As one kills vermin, we kill Jews.'

"But, it takes a very, very committed person to be able to believe those kind of lies. What about the simple guard in Auschwitz? What about the young fellow who just went along with the crowd? He didn't really believe that stuff. In his heart he knew it was all garbage. So what does he answer to that Voice Inside that screams out and says:

'What are you doing, Hanz, what is going on here?! This is Genocide and you are a part of it. Stop! Stop right now. Better to jump into that pit of fire yourself then to throw in one more innocent child.'

"He had to answer, he had to say something. So his answer was:

'Loyalty. Loyalty to Germany, loyalty to the party, loyalty to Der Führer. How can a nation of 80 million people be wrong? Maybe I don't know all of the answers, but The Führer is great and I must trust in Der Führer. I have a duty to my country and my people. Therefore I must do it. I must follow orders.'

"You see, Susan, the Voice was there, he knew in his heart this was a heinous, barbaric and evil crime against humanity. In his heart he knew this, and he couldn't live with that. No human being could. So, he had to make a choice, either don't do it, or find some way of explaining it. Find some way that makes it better, that excuses it, that at least explains away that awful feeling of guilt that rests inside his human heart. So they did just that, they either made the choice that so few made: to rebel, and fight against the very culture they had been brought up in, or they bought into the lines. They swallowed up the trash the ministry of propaganda was serving that day, and assuaged their conscience with bunk.

"Whatever we may think about these people, they were humans. If we put them into the category of inhuman monsters, we actually take away a level of culpability from them. They were human, and that is what makes them responsible for what they did. Every last one of them was guilty of the most horrific crimes imaginable to man. To allow them to do this, there had to be a system, a system that allows a human being, the height of creation, to willingly, knowingly commit demonic acts that we don't have words to describe. For this to happen, there had to be built into man this ability to believe whatever he wants to, whether it makes any sense or not.

"I don't think that in the course of history you will ever find a man, who set his course to be evil. I don't think a human being ever existed who said, *'I am evil, and wish to perpetrate wrong doings.'* Quite the opposite, everyone, no matter how depraved, no matter how far down the ladder of morality they sank, felt that what they were doing was right, that what they were doing was good. It had to be that way, because of the very manner in which God created man; man can't do 'bad.'

"So where does that leave us? If every path we set out upon will become good in our minds, regardless of whether it is or isn't; if every choice that we make ends up being proper, because we have this inborn capacity to make everything right—how does a human truly know if their choices are moral and proper? Even more, how are we to find our path in this maze that we call life?

"To help us in this quest, God gave us the Torah, the one universal set of standards against which we can measure ourselves. Standards that don't change with the times, and aren't subject to interpretation based on our whims or moods. Standards that withstand the test of time, because they were written to be eternal. Standards that aren't prey to the passing winds of social reform, which views today's ideas as progressive, and by tomorrow disparage them as antiquated.

"Since the Torah was written by our Creator, it is made up of universal codes, fundamental truths, and immutable laws that guide us through the tempest of uncertain social change. These allow us to chart our course in life, whatever winds are blowing in the social air of our times. They allow us to see through the darkness of this world and reach truths, real truths, hard core truths that last through the ages, helping us see past our own biases and desires.

"It is the program that allows that part of us, which fundamentally understands and only wants to do what is right in life, to surface, and gain primacy. Following the ways of the Torah brings a person to the heights of perfection. It is the one prescription that God wrote for the perfection of man. It is the one formula for man's success, to bring forth all that is great in man, allowing him to reach that potential for which he was put on this planet. We only need to reach out for the Torah and study its ways.

Chapter 20: I'll Never Die

I won't grow up, no I won't grow up.
I will never wear a tie; no I'll never wear a tie.
Or a serious expression, not a serious expression,
in the middle of July, in the middle of July.
No, I won't grow up, no I won't grow up, not I.
—Peter Pan

"David, do you remember the song in Peter Pan, *I Won't Grow Up?*"

"Rabbi, I have to admit that it's been a while."

"I find one point of particular interest in that song, the last lyric: '*No, I won't grow up not I.*' I find it telling because this is how the immature mind thinks. *The way it is now, is the way it will always be. The present state will continue on unchanged, forever'*. Even if you confront an immature person with the facts, and they fully accept them as true, it doesn't affect their mental state of being.

"Picture this in your mind. It's a beautiful spring day. Little Tommy, a second grader, doesn't want to go to school; he wants to stay home and play. Here's what the conversation sounds like:

Son: *"Mommy, I don't want to go to school."*

Mother: *"Tommy, you have to go to school. If you don't go to school, when you grow up, you won't be able to get a good job, and then you won't have enough money to buy a house, food, and all the other things that you will need. So, I want you to be a good boy, get your jacket on and get ready for the school bus."*

"What do you think little Tommy's reaction is going to be?

Son: *"Oh Mommy, I never thought of it in those terms, you are so right, I must get good grades so I can get into a good college, so I can get into the Masters Program I am interested in, and so I can buy a nice home in the suburbs. I will get my coat on right now."*

"Somehow I don't think so. In fact, in our little scenario Mother couldn't be more off the mark. First off, little Tommy has no real plans for ever being an adult. In his mental reality, he will always be a little child, and his Mommy and Daddy will always be there. And, even if Tommy had the understanding that one day he will grow up, there is no way that he has the emotional maturity to begin the process of building credentials for something that is over twenty years away. But it doesn't matter anyway, *"Because Mommy and Daddy will always be there to take care of me"*.

"You see, the signs of maturity are demonstrated by two criteria. One is emotional fortitude that allows me to push off immediate gratification for a later good. The other measure of maturity is the ability to see the big picture. One of the prominent differences between the mature and immature person, is an ability to see the future happening. The mature person is able to put off today for a better tomorrow, because he sees tomorrow as coming, to the immature mind tomorrow—if it will ever come—might as well be a millennium from now.

"For quite some time now, it has been an accepted point of view, that children aren't simply adults with short bodies. Their emotional fabric is different. Their entire emotional operating system is unlike that of an adult's. The underlying difference has a lot to do with being able to see the future as if it were here now. To be able to plan for events that are far off. To be able to see the consequences of my actions, not only here, in the immediate present, or tomorrow, next week, next month, but to be able to look to the future. To be able to clearly see what will come about next year, five years from now, ten years from now. The more immature a person, the more they live in the immediate present. To a child, there is nothing, nothing more valuable in the world, right now, then that shiny red fire truck with the working siren and whistle.

"Ask a five year old, *"Son, would you rather have a $1,000 or the fire truck?"*

"It's not even a contest! Many well-intending grandparents have met with disappointment at their grandchild's reaction, when the child found out that year's Chanukah present was an investment in a mutual fund. The child doesn't care, because the child isn't thinking about the future. Children live for right now. Their mood swings can be so great because right now the greatest thing in the world just happened, and ten minutes later the worst possible situation in the whole world can come about, when they find out they are not going out for pizza, as promised.

"As a person matures, he is able to see more into the future, seeing themselves in other settings, seeing themselves in different roles, and more significantly, the future is real to them. It is no longer a theoretical notion that they will one day have to get a job. It is real. It is me, the very same person who sits here right now, will be responsible to make ends meet. That sense of seeing the future as if it were here now, feeling emotionally that it really is going to happen, is a function of maturity.

"This concept of maturity, and with its resulting widening of one's sight, the ability to cast into the future, doesn't depend upon how smart or educated a person is. A person can have a very high IQ, and be able to perform brilliant mental feats, yet have the maturity of a twelve year old. Even when we find the occasional child prodigy, whose mental faculties are on the level of a twenty year old, their temperament is still that of a 10 year old, and they still behave like a child. Maturation is a process that often comes with age. Like a wine that ferments, the human mind, with age, acquires a certain ripening, a maturing, a broader view. Wisdom goes hand in hand with maturity. The wisdom to see the net results of my actions, the wisdom to see what this course will bring me to.

"To many of the classic Jewish thinkers one of the measures of wisdom is how far a person can see into the future—not in a clairvoyant, supernatural manner, but as a consequence of insight and analysis. If you do this, it will lead to that, which will lead to this, which will lead to that...

"When Rabbi Yosef Ber Soleveichik became known as one of Jewry's leaders, he was heard lamenting the loss of his father, the famous Rabbi Chaim Soleveichik. *The world doesn't know what it has lost. My father could see fifty years into the future, and me, I can barely see ten years forward'.*

"To me one of the most important manifestations of this concept of maturity and ability to see the future as being real, is our attitude towards dying—not death in general, but towards our own death.

"David, let me ask you a question. Do you plan on dying?"

"I can't say that I spend a lot of time thinking about it, except in our sessions," David quipped, "But, I am certainly aware that I am human, and my time will come. All the same, I plan on being here for a good long time."

"Let me share a story with you," I said. "My mother-in-law was in the kitchen one hectic Friday afternoon cooking, cleaning, preparing for the Sabbath. The phone rang; it was a telemarketer, selling, of all things, grave stones. He started his pitch.

'Ma'am, we offer the finest grave stones, made from imported marble, guaranteed not to weather.....'

"My mother-in-law answered in a low calm voice, *'It won't be necessary, I don't plan on dying.'*

'Madam, I don't mean to be morbid, but we all must go one day,' he responded.

'Yes, I understand, but I don't intend to die.'

'Madam,' he responded, 'Surely you know that your time too shall come.'

'I guess you didn't hear what I said. I have no intention of dying. Thank you,' and she ended the conversation.

"While my mother-in-law said that line in jest, there is a lot of truth in it. We don't really intend to die. We certainly are aware that it will happen, but it doesn't enter into our operating thoughts. Intellectually we know that we will die, but emotionally it remains in some distant far off place, and we certainly don't live our lives as if they will ever end.

"I have met many a person who is so responsible in all areas of their life, planning things so carefully. Putting away money for retirement, buying life insurance just in case, disability insurance, because *'Hey, you never know','* setting up annuities for the grandchildren—who aren't even born yet. Everything all planned for, all arranged, every element of life in place, down to the minutest detail. Except for one little area they forgot to deal with: what happens at the end of it all?

"If, in fact, you really saw yourself dying, wouldn't you think that you would spend some serious time thinking about this subject? You didn't leave your retirement up to chance. You didn't say, *'We'll worry about it when we get there.'* You worked out every last particular, *'What if I die first, then the estate goes to my wife, there is a tax advantage. If she dies first then her half goes to the kids, in a trust fund...'* No stone was left unturned. Expect this one little detail. This one little minutia that might be the single most important thought in your entire existence; what happens after I die? What then?

"The reason for this is that we don't really see ourselves ever dying. On one level we know it—after all, how many people do you know, who shook hands with George Washington? How many people can say they met Abraham Lincoln? I may even be able to quote the rate of death for men of my age and general health, but all of that remains in theory. In my emotional realm, in my real mode of functioning, it will never happen.

"We have this amazing capacity to totally block out this reality from our emotional operating mode. We are almost not equipped to deal with this reality, '*What do you mean, I won't be here anymore? I won't exist? I have always existed. My entire life I have been here. Where else will I be but here?*' Intellectually, we can understand the concept of death, we can discuss it, it makes sense. It is on an emotional level that we just can't relate to it really happening. The truth is, that for most of us death remains a theoretical concept, not one that we really accept that will ever happen to us.

"There is a deep-rooted reason for this phenomenon. When we spoke about God creating man in a manner that allows for Free Will, we made the observation that the only way to do this, was to keep a fair playing field, where it is as easy to do bad as to do good. Since man was created with a Spiritual Soul, God balanced it by putting the power of imagination in man. Now, that he can 'believe what he wants to believe,' he is free to choose, and is now free to shape himself. To maintain this balance ,another element had to be added to the human character: the inability to really see ourselves dying. If I was totally logical about life, and saw an end to my days, not in a theoretical, intellectual manner, but for real; if I could vividly and graphically see that my tenure on this earth will come to an end, and my current state will cease to be—that understanding would so skew the entire process of living that it would no longer be an even playing field.

"I would be forced to deal with issues that would radically change the way that I approach life. I would be forced to confront this most vital issue of what the purpose of my life is. What am I doing here? What is my goal? How could I possibly live my life for silly and frivolous pursuits if in fact I see that it will shortly come to an end? That reality alone would force me to ask the question of why? Why am I here, what is my purpose? What am I supposed to accomplish? And I couldn't possibly live my life in slumber as I do now.

"Don't you see, David, we are sound asleep. We live our lives with so little forethought, so little attention, so little concentration on what we are doing. We just go on. We follow that track that was set many years ago, hoping, praying, that it is the right path. But we don't know. We don't know, because we never asked the question. We don't know, because we never thought about the issue. We just go on, like a man asleep, like a drunk in his stupor; we go on through life without a care in the world.

"Oh, don't get me wrong, we do care, we have very real cares about all of those important and significant details that make up the substance of our life. Being here, doing this, taking care of this and getting through that. Most of all doing, doing, doing! We are so darn busy doing things. Isn't it amazing that one detail, one issue, the purpose of it all, we are just to busy too deal with?

"You see, if we were to come face to face with this issue, if we would ever be gut-wrenching, brutally honest with ourselves and ask: why am I doing all of this? What is the purpose of it all? Then we would find a very different perspective on life. If we were forced to confront this issue in a real manner, as if it was really going to happen to us, as if we will one day really leave this earth—that awareness alone would change the whole balance of life. That part of us, our Spiritual Soul, would demand, *'Do something! Contribute, accomplish. You only have a short while here. Discover your purpose, and darn it, pursue it for all that you are worth.'*

"If I was totally alert, if I only existed in a state of clarity of thought, and understood that every action of my life shapes the person that I will be for eternity, not some alter ego, not some distant cousin, but me; if I truly saw that "I" will leave my current state and live on forever, as I have shaped myself—then, of course that understanding would vastly change the playing field. To do something improper would be like putting my hand in a fire, something that, in theory, I have Free Will to do, but never would.

"The result would be that there would be no balance. To allow for Free Will, to allow man to choose his path and get credit for molding himself, by definition, it has to be easy to lose one's way. It has to be easy to get so caught up in the process of living that we would just sleep our time away, without ever asking or dealing with the most basic of all issues.

"That is why it is so difficult for us to find our path in life. That is the battle for which we were placed on this earth. That is the struggle that we will be given credit for winning. That is the shaping of the person. If the path were clear, if the way were easy to find, then our lives would be that of automaton, creatures preprogrammed to do only good. We would be capable of doing bad—but not dumb enough to actually go ahead with it. So where is Free Will, where is the challenge, where is the growth that comes from choosing 'good?'

"For that reason God created us in this state of the semi-mature, where certain thoughts and recognitions elude us. Most of all, the recognition that our lives, as we live it, will come to an end, is almost beyond our scope of thought.

"Rabbi Israel Meir Kagan, known as the Chofetz Chaim, one of the leaders of WWI Jewry, put it this way: in our hearts we feel as if there is a special society of people who die. It is the older people who die, people who are sick, or those unlucky ones, a select group, and I am not a member of that society.

"I remember visiting my grandmother when she was in her mid-eighties. She stayed in a hotel for the summer, and I would drive up to visit. On one occasion, we were sitting with her friends, all people close to her age group, and one of the women said something like, *'Isn't it a shame how the old people are dying?'* David, most of these women were over eighty!

"I was dumb struck. These were elderly people, all grandmothers, all had lost mothers and fathers, many had lost younger siblings, most of these women were themselves widows. Of course they were very aware the didn't have that much time left. But it still remained in a certain sense theoretical. It wasn't real. It still resided, on a certain level, as something that wasn't going to happen to them. They couldn't see past that blind spot of human thinking—that they, too, will die.

"To me one of the clearest examples of this is teenage smoking. Smoking is a habit that millions of Americans wish they would never have acquired. I don't think that you will ever meet a smoker who says, *'Oh yes, I am so glad that I began this death process, one that ruins my health, makes me feel sick, and is annoying to me and everyone around me.'* Most people curse the day they began. Yet I am constantly amazed, as I pass the local public high school, to see groups of teenagers, boys and girls, many with cigarettes in their hands.

"I live in a nice suburb; the kids in the school all come from good families. These are bright, nice kids, all having been indoctrinated with the finest we can provide in drug-free education, and yet there they are smoking. Why? Don't they get it? Don't they understand, this is a habit that is self destructive? Don't they know that they are damaging themselves with every breath they take? Why do they do it?

"Common wisdom tells us: *'They are giving into peer pressure, they want to seem very grown up, adult like. It is rebelliousness; a part of them finding themselves, asserting their independence.'* All of the lines that we are accustomed to hearing. I want you to think about this: with all of the peer pressure in the world, would a sane, rational person, do something to damage himself? Would these same teenagers take a knife and cut off a limb? Would they inflict harm upon themselves? I know many of them; they are intelligent, sensitive young people. They can even quote the exact statistical percentages of death from tobacco related diseases in their age bracket. Yet they smoke.

"What is actually going on in the teenage mind is that they don't emotionally accept that this activity will be damaging to them. They might spout to you all kinds of facts about the higher rate of emphysema amongst smokers, the increased chances of heart attack, the greater occurrence of lung cancer. That is all good and well, on paper, *'But it won't happen to me. I'll just quit before it gets bad. I have plenty of time. Don't worry about me; I can take care of myself.'* Or more accurately, what is actually going on in their mind is *'I'll never grow up, I will never be an old person. It won't happen to me.'* Of course, no sane teenager would ever mouth these kinds of lines, because in our conscious mind we all know them to be absurd, but there is more that shapes our behavior then just the rational, sane mind.

"In a similar vein, even mature adults are unable to focus on death. The reason for this is, much like the immature mind, we are incapable of staying focused on the really big picture. For that reason, I think there is a third term that we should use: the super-mature. To me, that connotes someone who has the complete balance, who is living in this world but is aware of the greater purpose of it.

"Such people are able to see what they do on this earth as important, very important—but they see it fitting into a grander scheme of things. They have the totality of the picture. Not only in an intellectual sense, as some memorized fact, but as something that is real to them, something they feel, something that effects the way they act, think, and how they approach all elements of life. They live with the knowledge that, we are here for a few short years, we have a very real and important mission on this earth, and then we will leave. "I", me, not someone else, not my alter ego, me.

"This emotional perspective changes every element of their lives. Everything takes on a different, more significant meaning. This single mind shift changes their life, as no other thought possibly could. Life itself becomes precious. Their time becomes so meaningful. Even their suffering becomes become significant, as it fits into a greater plan. They see themselves as babies born in this world, they see themselves here as they are now, and they see themselves after they have left this world. This is one of the most empowering concepts that a human can come to.

"David, I want you to understand, this isn't an easy goal, to move our lives into a state of super-maturity, to have a true world view of our life.

"As we discussed, this isn't an intellectual exercise. It isn't a question of acquiring some new information, it isn't an issue of our studying some texts, getting the correct life's perspective and then whammo; Everything changes. It is much more like a maturation process. We are dealing with an inner condition change, one, where we have to change our emotional makeup. It is a process, a growth process, and one that takes a lot of time and work. It takes a lot of thinking, a lot of dwelling upon these ideas, and it takes constant reinforcement. Even after we have been exposed to the viewpoint, and are intellectually comfortable with our purpose in this world, we tend to forget. We still have a tendency to lose sight of the big picture.

"Rabbi Israel Salanter, who is known as the father of the Mussar movement, had many close disciples who followed in his ways. One of his primary teachings was this very point, the importance of keeping focused on one's purpose in this world.

"One of his students left Poland, traveled to Paris, and became a successful businessman. The report came back to Rabbi Salanter, that, while this student was quite successful in his business ventures, he was neglecting his religious pursuits. It wasn't long thereafter that Rabbi Salanter had occasion to travel to France. When this student heard about his Mentor's arrival, he immediately set out to meet him.

"At the train station, when Rabbi Salanter disembarked, the student stood anxiously waiting. He greeted his revered teacher, and after exchanging a few civilities, he asked Rabbi Salanter, *'What brings the master to Paris?'*

"Rabbi Salanter responded, *'Oh, I need to have a button sewn on my coat.'*

"This great man wasn't known to engage in jocularity, so the student was taken aback.

"Surely the Rabbi didn't hear my question, he assumed. So he repeated, *'What brings the Rabbi to France?'*

"Rabbi Salanter answered, *'I have heard that there are some very fine tailors in Paris, and, as I mentioned, I need a button sewn on my coat.'*

"The student didn't know what to say other than, *'Surely there are enough tailors back in Poland, that the Rabbi didn't have to make such a long, difficult trip, solely for the purpose of sewing on a button.'*

"To which Rabbi Salanter responded. *'You can't believe that I would make such a long and arduous trip for something as trite as sewing on a button. Yet your soul has made a much longer journey to come to this world, and you live as if you were put here to make money.'*

"Powerful words, insightful words, spoken out of love and concern, penetrating to the core of this man's existence.

"David," I said, "let's understand what was happening. This student was a mature man, quite successful as well. He had spent his youth growing in spirituality under the guidance of one of the greatest teachers of the generation. He didn't lack any intellectual understanding about the purpose of life. He had studied this subject, delved into it, spent many years involved in it; yet his life, as he was living it now, didn't reflect that understanding. Not because he didn't see it clearly, not because of any questions that he had about it, but because he got so absorbed in the business of life, that he lost focus of the reason behind it all.

"What Rabbi Salanter was providing was a wake up call, to remind his student of what he knew, but what was no longer a part of his operating mode.

"What he was saying was, *'I am not here to tell you anything new; these are points that you understand only too well. The problem is that you haven't taken the time of late to dwell on them; to ponder them, to allow them to shape your behavior and life.'*

"You see, David, everything that we have been speaking about until now is meaningless, if it doesn't bring change. If a person studies these concepts, and says 'Now I have a further understanding about life,' but lives his life the same way he did up until that point, then clearly he didn't get the message. Because the message, while it may focus on death, is about life. Not in the abstract, not in some philosophical discussion about the meaning of life, but in a very real concrete manner—focusing, altering, improving. The most powerful lesson that death has to offer us, is how to live life. When a person has a near death experience, life itself becomes so much more precious. When a young woman is diagnosed with cancer, every moment of her life remaining becomes charged with significance. Why? What changed? Only one key focal point. She now sees in a very real way, that her life will in fact come to end. For the first time in her existence, she finally gets it. It finally, finally comes through. She is going to die, and that focus changes everything.

"Why does it have to wait until a person gets a tragic prognosis? Why does it have to wait until it's too late to do anything about it? If we could focus on death, on our death, then our life would be totally different. Our lives would be so much more directed, so much more passionate, so much more meaningful. We would be able to live our life by design, not by chance, and we would be so much more alive."

Chapter 21: Frank and Joe

"David," I said, "we humans have a tendency to get so caught up in the details of life that we lose site of where we are headed. Many times we get into situations, and before we even realize what has happened to us, we are way down the garden path, down a path we never intended to be on. Then it is too late. We stand there wondering how did this happen? How did I get here? How did I ever get so caught up? But that is a reality of life. We become creatures of habit, and before we know it, we are in it deep, and we don't know how to get out.

"I recently read an essay by a Jewish woman, grappling with the problem that her husband, who is Catholic, wants to bring a Christmas tree into their home. She couldn't quite identify why a tree in her house bothered her so, but it did. It left her without peace. She mentioned all of the different solutions that she had discussed with her friends. Maybe putting a Jewish Star on top. Only using blue and white decorations (the colors of Israel). Having Santa leave Chanukah Gelt under the boughs as gifts. But of course, none of these solutions satisfied her ultimate confusion, and Chanukah, the holiday of light brought her only darkness.

"What aggravates her dilemma tenfold is that her children are in the middle of this conflict. While her husband has agreed to bring them up as Jews, there is constant confusion. On Passover we eat Matzo, on Yom Kippur we fast, on Christmas we gather around a tree. You could almost hear the desperation in her unspoken cry of '*How did I end up here?*'

"Keeping in mind, this is an intelligent, sensitive woman, I can guarantee she did not plan to get herself into this situation, it just happened. She met a guy, a nice guy, as it turned out he was an honest, caring and sensitive man, and they started bonding. A normal course of affairs.

"What she didn't realize back then was that she was making a decision. She was unwittingly deciding to put herself into this situation. This situation that resulted in her children's father being Catholic, and now finding herself in a dilemma that she can't resolve.

"That is life. Many of our crucial decisions happen that way. It is rare that we actually choose our path. We sort of go about this business of living, and what happens, happens. We meet a person, get involved with a certain group, find ourselves spending time with these people, and life goes on. It usually isn't until years later that we wake up and find ourselves somewhere, wondering how we got there.

"If you study substance abusers, you will find that for many it begins as a simple kick. A friend turns them on to alcohol or drugs, and they find it has an appeal. It's fun. So they do it again. *Why not? Who's hurt? What's the damage?* Theoretically, if a person could remain an occasional, recreational drug user, the damage wouldn't be that severe. The problem begins with that slow and insidious habit that begins forming. Every time they come home from work, *they need a drink.* Or, every time something difficult happens in their life, *they need to get high.* It begins slowly at first, then little by little, until this person, a regular person, a person just like you or me, finds himself addicted—a slave to the bottle, pills, or cocaine. Then he wonders, *'How did I get here? How did this happen? How did I let myself get to this point?'*

"The answer is, they never just got there. They never just found themselves at this point. It was a long and gradual road—it was a long slip down the slope, and the whole way down they never knew which way they were headed. David, no one ever decides to be a drug addict, a wife beater, a criminal, or any of the sociopaths that we read about in the papers. Life takes its course, and they proceed, it is only long after they are down that path, once it is too late, that they wake up and find out where they are.

"To show you what I mean, I would like to share another parable with you.

"Frank and Joe go way back. They were roommates in college. They haven't seen each other since they left school, but Frank often finds himself thinking back on those old days. Throughout their college years Frank felt sort of bad for his friend Joe. Joe was a decent guy, but when everyone else was out partying and having a good time, there was *Joe the Loser* studying. It seemed that Joe studied morning and night, you almost never saw the guy without a book in his hand. While everyone else was out there getting drunk, having a great time, there was *Joe the Loser,* sitting over the books. He didn't even have a girlfriend or anything. Poor guy.

"After graduating college, Frank and Joe went their separate ways. Joe graduated top in his class, went on to medical school, and became a well-established surgeon. And Frank, well... Frank sort of drifted. He graduated college with straight C', and could never find a job that he really liked. So, there he was working behind a fish counter in a grocery store.

"As fate would have it, the two meet up many years later, when Joe drives up to the parking lot of the supermarket. He parks his fancy, imported sports car, steps out and buttons his $1,500 dollar, custom made suit. As he walks into the store, who does he see working behind the fish counter? None other than his old buddy Frank.

'Frank, old buddy how are you doing?'

'Hey, Joe, is that you?'

'Wow, Frank. Been so long! How are you?'

'Great, it's been a long time! Wow, Joe, you sure look different. Is that a custom made suit? It looks great!'

'Yeah, just got it, and Frank, You look, um, different... I really like your... oh, I mean your apron,' Joe responds.

'Hey, Joe, what you driving these days?'

'Well I sort of just picked up this new Italian sports car...'

'And you, Frank, what are you driving these days?'

'Well I'm driving this old hunker, just until I can afford something better.'

'Listen, old buddy, really great seeing you.'

'Yeah you too, Joe. Maybe we'll get together to talk about old times.'

'Sounds great, give me a call.'

"At that moment it hits Frank—the recognition comes crashing through. He realizes that his friend has it all. He works four days out of seven, plays golf two afternoons a week, lives in a custom made home, is happily married with one child and another on the way, and is active in the community. More than that, Joe is doing something with his life, something important and significant. And, here is Frank, thirty something, working behind a fish counter making a little over minimum wage, driving a beat up old jalopy, living in a one bedroom apartment. and going nowhere. At that moment it hits him like a ton of bricks:

'What a jerk I was. How could I possibly be so stupid? What an opportunity I wasted. All those years that I use to look at Joe as the loser, and now look at him.'

"But, it isn't just at this moment that Frank will bemoan his fate. For the rest of his life, every time that he has to make a mortgage payment, or his beat up old car breaks down, or one of his kids say to him, *'How come my friends get to go on vacation with their parents, and we never go anywhere?'* he will kick himself. Every time he wakes up in the middle of the night wondering, why he is caught up in this dead end job going nowhere, doing nothing, not contributing, not producing, just wasting away. Throughout his life, over and over, he will come back to this one realization: *'I blew it. I had the chance. I could have made myself into something, and I didn't. I could have really been someone and now look at me. Why? Not for any good reason, but because I got caught up in all of the stupid, passing things going on around me. I lost focus on why I was in school in the first place.'* Over and over again the same haunting lyric will play in his mind:

'If only I could go back in time, and do it over again.'

"But he can't, he had his shot, he had his one go around, and he blew it. Now for the rest of his life he will be what he made of himself.

"David, this is a parable to life. A parable that is so powerful, that if we take it to heart, it could literally change our lives. You see, whether we want to admit it or not, we are all a little like Frank. We tend to get caught up in all that goes on around us. Blame it on human nature, call it part of being a social being, but we tend to mimic whatever is going on around us. We get caught up in the here and now and lose sight of the big picture. Whatever is going on around us we start doing ourselves. If the society we live in values money, that becomes important to us.

"If we live amongst people whose self-worth is directly tied to their net worth, it affects us, and it starts getting in our way of thinking. Even though in my heart it's not really me, I get dragged along. If we started with certain standards of behavior, and those around us don't value them, we tend to compromise. Not wittingly, not immediately, but slowly over time, in the slippery slope of life, we begin melding into the surrounding moral landscape. That's just the way we humans are.

"David, do you remember when we discussed that the Vilna Gaon teaches us that the most painful moment in a person's life is after they die, when they no longer confined to their body, no longer blinded by all of the physical trappings of this world? At that moment they can see life with a totally clear vision. Then when they hold up a picture of this great person and say, why isn't that *you*? That is what *you* could have become had *you* used *your* life as it was meant to be used. That is *you* as *you* were destined to be.

"The reason that this is the most painful moment in a person's life is because the "I" becomes overwhelmed with an irrepressible drive to go back. *'Please! Please! Please! Just give me one more chance. Just one more opportunity to spend some time working, improving, changing myself. Please!'* But then it is too late, life is over. This one chance at change, the one opportunity to grow is gone. The way *you* are at that moment in time is the way *you* will be for eternity. That realization, that *you* could have been so much greater, that *you* could have accomplished so much more, is the most tragic, heart rending moment in a person's existence.

"Let us go back to our parable for a moment. Let's imagine that just at that moment, when Frank hits that lowest point of his life, a voice from Heaven comes out and says:

'Frank, how would you like to go back in time? Go back to being eighteen. Just starting out in college. You would have the same opportunity, now with a fresh start, a new beginning. The chance to do it all over again.'

"Knowing Frank, we would expect him literally to scream out, *'Of course! I would do anything to go back. I am much wiser now, I understand things more clearly and I am much more sensible. There is no doubt in my mind, I now have the maturity to apply myself fully. Please give me this one chance. I am certain that I will succeed!'*

Unfortunately, Frank wasn't listening very carefully. The heavenly voice didn't offer to take thirty two year old Frank back in time. It didn't offer to take him as he is now, now that he is much more in control of his desires and far better at resisting distractions. It offered to take him back to when he was eighteen—with the same set of circumstances: the same impetuousness, the same desires, the same lack of responsibility.

Frank still says, *Yes, I'll do it!'*

"Let's imagine that we get to watch Frank transported back in time, back to being eighteen years old, back to the college campus. Still as immature, but this time Frank is ready. He is in his own words 'psyched for success.'

"The first thing Frank does when he appears back on campus is to go to the college book store. *'Hey, school starts in just ten days; it's never too early to be prepared.'* Books, notepads, daily planners, pens, our Frank is clearly a changed man.

"The first few weeks we do see a different person. Hard at work, studying, taking notes in class, you wouldn't recognize the old boy.

"It's been three straight weeks now of taking copious notes, getting into bed early, getting up early to study. Our man is poised for success.

"Then, Sunday night his old friend from High School, Harry comes by.

'Hey Frank, old buddy, how you doin'?'

'Hey, good seeing you, Harry.'

'Listen, Frankie boy, some of the guys are getting together tonight. You know, we've been in school over three weeks now, we figured, that was cause for a celebration.'

'Well, Harry I don't know...'

'Come on Frank, don't be a geek! Nothing crazy, just some guys getting together, see you later, old buddy?'

"Frank says to himself. *'What's the harm? Just some guys getting together to have a beer or two.'* So he joins his old friends.

"When Frank wakes up the next day for class, well... you just can't expect a person to function at his best when he's hung over, and going on three hours of sleep. So Frank kind of dozes off during the major lecture of the week. But don't worry; our hero will be right back on his feet in no time. He is determined to succeed.

"Things kind of do get back on course, back to the routine. Copious notes. Early to bed, early to rise.

"Until Thursday morning science lab. There she is, that blond, the one the guys keep talking about. The one our buddy Frank has had his eye on for the past three weeks. Lo and behold, she is assigned to him as a lab partner. Well our hero is in seventh heaven. *'This is great! Just say the right line, time it right and she's mine,'* Frank is thinking to himself. Frank always was a smooth one, and things go along just as planned, he even gets her to agree to a date for Saturday night. Our man is set!

"Until he remembers that he was to meet Joe on Saturday night to study. Joe always was the studious one, never one to miss an opportunity to get a head start on next week's assignments. Since his metamorphous, Frank has been studying with Joe every Saturday night. *'Well,'* Frank says to himself, *'I am absolutely committed to doing this school thing right, but how can I miss out on this opportunity? No problem. I'll do both! I'll go out with her on Saturday night, and study by myself on Sunday. Who says you can't have it all?!'*

"Well, our super hero does even better than expected. I mean, this girl likes him, really likes him. It's not just that he is so cool; she is so impressed with how serious he seems to be about life.

She never met an eighteen year old guy with such direction, such a sense of where he's going.

'What could be better?' Frank says to himself. *'Here I am, I have everything, I'm serious about life, I have a real direction, and I get the best girl on campus, too. Life could not be better.'*

"As it turns out, the date went a little later then expected. While he had promised himself to be back in his room by midnight, it wasn't until somewhere after 3:00 A.M., that he actually made it back. *'But hey, not a problem, now that my love life, is settled, I will have even more focus on my studying.'* Frank sets his alarm for 8:00 A.M.

"Our friend gets out of bed the next morning. Well, not quite at 8:00 AM., and not quite in the morning, but by 1:00 PM, he is showered, fresh and ready to begin a hard day, (well, afternoon) of intense studying. He lays out his books, pulls out his notes and starts plugging away.

"To be honest, things aren't going quite as Frank would like them to be. You see, that one lecture that he missed was a lot more important then he realized. In fact, most of what he is studying now doesn't make any sense to him. But our Frank is determined, there is no way that he is going to lose this one golden opportunity of life. Not him. No way! So Frank doggedly plows on. Until his cell phone rings.

'Hi Frank?'

'Yes.'

'It's me, Barbara.'

'Oh, hi, Barbara.'

'Frank, I wanted to tell you, I had a really nice time last night.'

'I did also, Barbara.'

'Well Frank, that is why I wanted to talk to you, there is something very important that I need to speak to you about, do you think that I could come over now?'

'Well, I... I mean, I... Well you see, I kind of like... I mean, I have this major test tomorrow, and I am studying intensely.'

'Oh, I see...' her voice drops.

'Now, don't get the wrong idea. I mean, you know. It's not that I don't want to talk to you or anything. It's just this school thing. I have to study.'

'Frank I need to talk to you. It's real important. It won't take long.'

'OK, but please remember, I can't take too much time away from studying, okay?'

"Well, needless to say, our fearless hero didn't get much studying done, that day. Or the day after that, or the one after that either. For all of his new found determination and drive, it wasn't long before Frank ended up getting straight C's again, but what could he do?

"David, can you feel the power of this parable? Can you see how real it is? How similar to our own lives it really is? You see, that is us, even if we wake up, and we come to recognize the importance of life. Even if we come to understand this literally once in a lifetime opportunity to perfect ourselves. How can we succeed? We are human, and as humans we are weak and tend to fall asleep. We get caught up in things and before we know it, it is ten years later, twenty years later, and we don't even have a clue to how we got here.

"But, what can I do? How can I live my life any differently than I am doing now? I know how important life is. I understand that this is my one opportunity to grow, to accomplish. But I am so rooted in the way that I am, I've been this way all my life. Maybe had I been brought up differently? Maybe had I had a different focus on life? But this is where I am at now. What can I realistically do about it now? This is who I am.

"For that reason God gave us the Torah. He gave us a guidebook to live our life in this world. He gave us the one tried and true road to travel that will allow us to accomplish the task for which we were placed here. The Torah shows us how to chart our course, and how to find our path. It also warns us over and over again to keep mindful, to keep reading that book. Constantly study it, always review it, make it a part of your life—because even when we are on that path, we tend to forget. So we need to continually read and study it, and come to new understandings so that we don't lose sight of our purpose in being here.

"You see, while God put us on this planet to grow, He also put us in a situation where there are many things that pull us away from Him. That is the challenge of life and the reason we were put here on this earth. All of the physical manifestations that we get so busy with, that fill our days, pull us away from that ultimate goal. There is very little in our lives that actually pulls us closer to God, that actually strengthens our connection to Him. So it is easy for us to get so involved in this process we call living, that we forget there was supposed to be a purpose in the first place.

"For that reason, to help us find our way, to allow us to chart our course, and show us the way for the generations, God gave us the Torah, the Divine Directive. It shows us how to live, how to approach life, how to find meaning and direction in our stay on this planet. It was hand written by the source of all wisdom in this world. The source of knowledge and thought, our Creator, told us this is the solution. With it there is light, without it darkness. If our Creator Himself tells us, that without it we won't find our way, what are the odds of a person being successful without following the prescribed course?

"It is true that the Torah contains rules, rules for conduct, rules for living our lives—and by nature we hate rules. We yearn for freedom; we wish to be unshackled, not to have to follow any set patterns, or commands. But these are standards that not only allow us to reach our potential, they enhance our stay in this world. The ways of the Torah are pleasant. Not only in the sense that they allow us to follow a path of life, but because they were designed by our Creator, Who only wishes for our benefit, and wants us to enjoy every element of our life. Just like we find so much of God's creation custom fashioned for our benefit and enjoyment, so too, he gave us a system that will enhance our short stay in this world, and benefit us for eternity. Our job is to study that guide, make it part of our life, and bring our life up to standards listed in it.

Chapter 22: The Eternal People

Remember the days of yore,
study the years of each generation,
ask your father and he shall tell you,
your elders shall recount for you what passed.
(Deuteronomy 32)

"David," I said, "I want to tell you a story, I can't tell you that it actually happened, but there is much to be learned from it.

"It was the late 1920's; Hitler was beginning his rise to power, speaking in the beer halls of Munich. At one such meeting, amidst the haze of cigarette smoke and the smell of Bavarian beer, Hitler's voice could be heard ranting about Germany's problems.

'The misfortune of Germany is the Jews. The Jews are the reason we lost the war. The Jews are the reason we suffer unemployment. The Jews are the reason we have bread lines. The salvation of the German Fatherland rests on ridding ourselves of the Jews!'

"When he finally finished this hour-long tirade, the audience leapt to its feet in adoring applause.

"Towards the back of the room an old man, obviously Jewish, also stood up and clapped. Long after the rest of the audience finished applauding and began shuffling out, this old man continued his ovation.

"Hitler made his way over to the elderly gentleman and screamed, *'Don't you believe that I am serious when I say, the Jews are Germany's misfortune?! Don't you believe me when I say that I intend to rid Germany of the Jews?!'*

"The old man, undaunted, turned toward Hitler and said *'Oh, I assume that you meant every word of what you said. You must remember, though, we are an old people and you aren't the first to hate us. Many years ago there was an evil King Pharaoh who also hated us. He enslaved our people for over 200 years. God saved us from him, and in honor of that event we have the beautiful holiday of Passover. The entire family gets together and celebrates. What a joyous occasion! Many centuries later there was a wicked man named Haman. He also hated us, and tried to kill us. God saved us from him, and in honor of that experience we now have the festival of Purim. What a wonderful feast, singing and dancing. Then came the Greeks who tried to oppress us, and we now have Chanukah, marking that occasion. But you, Hitler, you hate us more than any of our enemies. When God saves us from you, what a rejoicing there will be!'*

"David, there is no holiday that marks God saving us from the Holocaust. There is no day of celebration. There are no family gatherings, there are no traditions reminding us of the salvation. But, we are still here. Despite the all-out efforts of the Nazi regime to systematically annihilate us, we are still here to talk about it. While the rest of the world turned their back in silence, one of the most powerful nations on the face of the Earth did everything in their power to destroy us. That bestial country unleashed all of its fury and hatred in one final solution to the Jewish problem. They couldn't do it, we are still here today. You and I are still sitting here, discussing our heritage, contemplating its meaning, while our enemies are relics of the past.

"Isn't it amazing, that century after century after so many repeated attempts to wipe out the Jewish people, that we are still here, and our enemies aren't?

"We are an ancient people. We have lived through 2,000 years of exile, being thrown out of every land in which we lived. Sent from exile to exile, barely accepted in some havens, only to be further oppressed and finally thrown out again. We have been subjected to every anguish and torment known to mankind. Starting with the destruction of the Second Temple almost 2,000 years ago, we have suffered through more ordeals than any other people on the face of the planet.

"We have lived through **Crusades, Spanish Inquisitions, Blood Libels, Pogroms, Persecutions, Mass murders, and Gassings.** Yet we are still here. Despite it all, we are still around to tell the tale, as vibrant and as strong as ever.

"We have a Passover because God saved us from Pharaoh. We have a Purim because God saved us from Haman. We have a Chanukah because God saved us from the Greek/Syrians. Even after the Holocaust—the most organized, systematic attempt in the course of history to eliminate a people—we are still here today. Where are our enemies who over and over again sought to destroy us? Where is the Egyptian empire now? Where are the Romans or the Greeks? All of the great empires have risen and fallen, and where are these people now? All of our enemies are gone and forgotten. We alone are left.

"Of all the ancient people the only one that remains intact, unchanged, still as alive as it ever was, is the Jewish Nation. The others had their moment of power, their star shone brightly for a time and faded. In their power and glory they attempted to crush us, to destroy us, and they failed. In their short-lived flash of might they too attempted to vanquish the Jew—they failed, and then faded from the face of history, never to be heard from again."

Reaching into my desk drawer I handed David a text book entitled, *The Jewish Dispersion* by Leschzinsky. I opened it to a page marked with a yellow post-it note and said, "Here, David, I would like you to read this."

'For 1,900 years from the destruction of the Second Temple (70 C.E.) to the establishment of the modern State of Israel (1948), the Jewish people have wandered literally around the world. This wandering was usually precipitated by intolerable spiritual and/or

physical persecution. The scope of the Jews nineteen-hundred-year exile is reflected in the lands from which they were, en masse, expelled. For example, in the third century (C.E.) they were expelled from Carthage (North Africa), in the fifth from Alexandria (Egypt), the sixth from provinces in France, and in the seventh from the Visigothic empire. In the ninth century they were expelled from Italy, in the eleventh from Mayence (Germany), in the twelfth from France, the thirteenth from England, the fourteenth from France, Switzerland, Hungary, Germany, and in the fifteenth from Austria, Spain, Lithuania, Portugal, and Germany. In the sixteenth and seventeenth centuries Jewish populations were expelled from Bohemia, Austria, Papal States, the Netherlands, the Ukraine, Lithuania, and Oran (North Africa). In the eighteenth and nineteenth centuries they were expelled from Russia, Warsaw (Poland), and Galatz (Romania). In the twentieth century all Jews living in Nazi controlled lands were relocated, and from 1948 to 1952 hundreds of thousands of Jews managed to escape from the lands of Egypt, Lebanon, Syria, and Iraq.'

"David," I said, "there was hardly a country that didn't expel us, and precious few places in which a Jew could find safe haven. Yet, with that being said, have you met anyone lately from the Visigothic Empire? What about the Roman Empire, or for that matter, the Greek/Syrian dynasty? They have come and gone, and the Jewish people alone are still around to talk about it. I challenge you to find a nation that was so disadvantaged, so discriminated against, so universally hated and oppressed for over 2,000 years. Yet of all of them, the only ones left intact and unchanged are the Jews.

"I want you to understand, this isn't my perspective because I'm a Rabbi, or even my perspective as a Jew, historians have also reached the conclusion that something is unique about this people. Here is an article written by Leo Tolstoy, in 1891, entitled *What is the Jew?*" Handing David a photocopy, I said "Here, why don't you read this.

'What is the Jew? This is not as strange question as it would first appear to be. Come, let us contemplate what kind of unique creature this is. Whom all the rulers, all the nations of the world have disgraced, crushed, expelled and destroyed; persecuted, burned and drowned, and who, despite their anger and fury, continues to live and flourish. What is this Jew, whom they have never succeeded in enticing with all the enticements in the world, whose oppressors and persecutors only suggested that they deny and disown this religion and cast aside the faithfulness of their ancestors?!

'The Jew—is the symbol of eternity. He is the one whom was never able to be destroyed, neither bloodbath, afflictions, fire nor the sword succeeded in annihilating him. He is the one who, for so long, has guarded the prophetic message and transmitted it to all mankind. A people such as this can never disappear. The Jew is eternal. He is the embodiment of eternity.'

"David, these are not the words of the Talmud quoted here. We aren't reading an article published by a Jewish thinker. These words were written by a man who viewed world history with the one criterion necessary to reach such an observation: an open mind. He studied the course of human events and in an unbiased posture reached the understanding that this people has a unique destiny, an eternal role in the ages.

"Here is another example,a student of world history reaching a similar conclusion. It was written by a French author, Jon DeBileda, during the latter part of the 19th Century.

'In essence, the Jewish people chuckle at all forms of anti-Semitism. Think all you want and you will not be able to find one form of brutality or strategy that has not been used in warfare against the Jewish people. I cannot be defeated, says Judaism. All that you attempt to do to me today has been attempted 3,200 years prior in Egypt. Then the Babylonians and Persians tried... the Romans, and then others...

'There is no question that the Jews will outlive us all. These are eternal people.... They cannot be defeated, understand this! Every war with them is a vain waste of time and manpower. Conversely, it is wise to sign a mutual covenant with them. How trustworthy and profitable they are as allies! [For instance] look at their patriotism, their commercial benefit, their ambition and success in science, arts, and politics! Be their friends, and they will pay you back in friendship one-hundred fold. This is an exalted and chosen people!'

"What strikes me," I said, "is that these weren't religious men; they weren't looking to find a redeeming perspective on Jewish suffering. They were historians, and their conclusion is: *This is an exalted and chosen people!'* Isn't that what we have been told by scriptures? Isn't that the point the Talmud tells us over and over again? Yet somehow it sounds even more powerful when it comes from the pen of people outside of the Jewish nation, coming from an objective and in some cases an antagonistic viewpoint.

"Here is something from one of our own, from one of the greatest Talmudic scholars of the 18th century, Rabbi Yonason Eybeschutz, a Rabbi, teacher and leader of his people. He writes:

'Will the atheist not be embarrassed when he reflects on Jewish history? We, an exiled people scattered sheep from antiquity, after all that we have brutally endured after thousands of years. There is no nation or people pursued as we. Many and powerful are those who aspired to totally destroy us, but they never prevailed. How will the wise philosopher respond? Is this extraordinary phenomenon truly by chance?'

"And one more comment from one of the Leaders of German Jewry, Dr. Isaac Breuer.

'The "People of the Book" among the nations is the most fantastic miracle of all, and the history of this people is literally one of miracles. One who sees this ancient people today, after thousands of years among the nations of the world, when he reads the Scripture

and finds that they prophetically relate clearly and simply to the ever-transpiring Jewish phenomenon, and does not fall on his face and exclaim "God, the Lord of Israel, He is God," then no other miracle will help him. For, in truth, this individual has no heart to understand, no eye to discern, and no ear to hear.'

"David," I said, "Even if we look at the most recent tragedy that has befallen the Jewish people, the Holocaust, with all of its brutality and barbarism, it couldn't accomplish the ultimate goal of its perpetrators; the *final solution* to the Jewish problem. Much to their eternal shame, we are still here. In Hitler's final address to his people, he laid out his policy towards the Jews.

'Above all I charge the leaders of the nation and those under them to scrupulous observance of the laws of race and to the merciless opposition to the universal poisoner of all peoples, international Jewry'.

"Hitler's vision was to set up a system of government to forge the way for generations to come. His Third Reich was to last at least one thousand years. Where are they now? And we, the sheep amongst the wolves, are still around telling the story.

"Still, I want you to realize that all of this, everything that we could possibly say about world history, pales in comparison to the miracle that we have witnessed with our own eyes in the last fifty years: the Jewish people in their country, the land of Israel. After an exile lasting almost 2,000 years, not only has this nation survived as a people, it has reclaimed a land that it left thousands of years ago—a land that was barren and desolate for centuries. Is there any thinking person who would call this short of miraculous? Is there any other nation in the course of history that was uprooted from its homeland and successfully made it back? We aren't speaking about returning after ten or twenty years of exile, but after almost 2,000 years of exile.

"Even more wondrous is that the Jews are still in that land some fifty years later; they weren't exactly welcomed back into their homeland. As soon as the state of Israel was declared, the Arab nations declared war. To the American Jewish community this meant disaster. When the word spread that the Arab nations were en masse attacking the fledgling State of Israel, common wisdom said: There will be another Holocaust. There was no way that such a small nation, so ill prepared for war, could possibly hold out against the organized effort of the entire Arab world.

"Just to give you a military perspective, look at this." I handed David a book entitled, *A History of the Jews,* by Paul Johnson opened to page 526.

'On May 14, 1948 the state of Israel was declared. The next day, five mechanized armies attacked; each one, alone, sizably larger than the small band of Holocaust survivors defending Israel.

The entire armament of the Israeli forces consisted of:

17,600 rifles
2,700 steno guns
1,000 machine guns
45,000 soldiers.'

"David," I said, "this is only part of the picture. Before the declaration of a state, Palestine was ruled by the British, and they had very strict rules against Jews owning guns. The fledgling Jewish guerrilla forces had to practice in great secrecy with minimal armaments and inadequate drills; without any of the normal machinations of an army. Much of the military training consisted of small groups gathering together in secret cells. This continued until May 14, 1948. On May 15th, five nations attacked. You can't create an army, a navy and an air force in one day.

"The entire Israeli Air force consisted of a few Piper Cubs that were originally loaded with grenades, and later fitted for machine guns. Each of the Arab nations alone had enough manpower and weapons to single-handedly defeat Israel. Can a nation so out manned, so out gunned, fighting not on one or two fronts, but on every side, possibly survive more than a few days? In 1948 less than five percent of Jews alive at the time lived in Israel. A total of 650,000 Jews were surrounded and attacked by nations populated by 50 million Arabs.

"Each attacking nation threw its full weight into the fray, coordinating their armies, mobilizing their tanks and heavy artillery, and sending their air force in for support, all galvanized for this one final attack.

"According to any intelligent assessment of the situation, there was to be a massacre. How could such a small, untrained band of men, with almost no previous military experience, possibly survive against the organized might of the Arab Nations, attacking them on every side?

"After one month a cease-fire was called. With all of the gathered might, they couldn't vanquish this little sliver of a country. You have to be amazed by the sheer unlikeliness of these events.

"I remember as a boy reading a book called, *The Birth of the Israeli Air Force*. One story described Jews, still under British rule, who began to fly single propeller airplanes on reconnaissance missions for the Haganah. Once the State of Israel was declared, and the Arabs proclaimed war, these Jews now became the Air Force. But their planes weren't fighters; they weren't equipped with guns, or bomb racks. The pilot would load a box of grenades behind his seat, fly low, and drop them on the Egyptian troops. This worked well until they ran out of grenades. So at this point as the famous story goes, one pilot thinks for a moment and asks for a case of soda bottles. His fellow soldiers thought he had gone insane, but he insisted. So when he takes off on his next mission, he has a case of soda bottles behind him. As he flies over the Egyptian troops, he drops a bottle; it hits the ground with a loud crash. The Egyptian soldiers, seeing a plane overhead and hearing an explosion, assume these were bombs, and run for their lives!

"Now this may be a charming story, but you don't win wars with soda bottles. You can't wage a war without arms, soldiers, tanks, or without artillery.

"Here is another story to give you a sense of what was going on.

"Bet Eshel was a small Kibbutz two miles outside of Beer Sheva. Near it, in the Negev, was a well-equipped Egyptian army base. Besides a full armament and infantry, they had garrisons of jeeps and tanks. When war was declared, the Kibbutzniks knew that they would be the first site attacked, so they prepared for the onslaught. They didn't have to wait long. The Egyptians began with a heavy artillery barrage. The settlers hunkered down in bunkers. They waited for the artillery attack to end and prepared themselves for the infantry assault that would surely follow. The Egyptian army attacked, charging in with more than 700 men. The fighting was fierce on both sides, yet the Kibbutzniks bravely fought them off. This entire garrison of trained professional soldiers could not take the Kibbutz. The truly amazing part was that at the time of the attack the arsenal of the Kibbutz consisted of twelve rifles and two machine guns!

"Fantasies aside, in the real world you can't fight off a garrison of soldiers with twelve rifles and two machine guns. Life just doesn't work that way. In the real world, people get killed, the strong survives, the better armed wins the war, and there is no way that Israel should have remained on the face of the map.

"The story reads like a fable. If you study the events, you have to assume that it couldn't really have happened that way. There must be some other explanation. But David, that is what happened, not long ago, but right in our day and age. No one expected the outcome as it happened. Certainly the Arab nations didn't.

"Azzah Pasha, then the Secretary General of the Arab League, proclaimed over the airwaves: *'This will be a war of extermination, and a momentous massacre.'* This is what everyone expected. This is what should have occurred according to all of the natural ways of the world.

"Over the next 40 years, the Arab states spent more than three times the amount of money on military weapons than Israel did. Keep in mind that this was during the cold war. Egypt and Syria had the full backing of the USSR not only in providing weapons, but in military training and strategy. Granted, the US provided help to Israel, but the scope of supplies and training didn't compare to what the Soviets were giving to the Arab block.

"Between 1948 and 1973, a span of 25 years, the Arab nations declared war four times on this puny, understaffed country; and not one victory.

"But none of this compares to the obvious and clear miracles that happened during the Six Day war in 1967.

"By this time there were three million citizens of Israel, surrounded by 100 million Arabs. It was so obvious that this was going to be a blood bath for the young state of Israel, that at the beginning of the war many of the Jewish day schools in the US held campaigns to gather bed sheets to be airlifted to Israel. Israel couldn't possibly have the medical supplies to care for all of the soldiers who would be wounded in the anticipated fighting, and the American Jewish community did what it could to help.

"Not only did Israel win the war with remarkably few casualties, they conquered huge tracts of the Sinai, took over the Golan Heights, and reclaimed Jerusalem. Within the first six hours almost the entire Egyptian Air Force was wiped out. After the war the Israeli intelligence uncovered something amazing. The Egyptians, being aware that Israel could bomb their air fields, had prepared decoy hangers. From the air Israeli planes saw two sets of hangers; one that housed the planes, and the decoys. After the war, they examined the hangers on the Egyptian air base; almost every hanger bombed was a direct hit. The empty decoy hangers were almost untouched; only the ones containing planes were destroyed.

"An article written in *Time* magazine after the war told the following story: '*the West Point Senior cadets were given a project. They were to devise the most effective strategy for taking the Golan Heights.*

'They were given maps of the Syrian strong points and the Israeli forces assigned to the battle. Because it was a senior thesis, they were given access to the greatest military minds at West Point, and the most sophisticated computers available at the time. They had three months to devise their strategy. Within a short time they returned to their professor saying it was not possible. Based on the sheer heights of the cliffs and the strength of the Syrian fortifications, it was not possible to plan the taking of the Golan Heights, because it just couldn't be done.'

"Yet it was done.

"What are we to say? Can a person deny what is so clear and obvious? Can a thinking person possibly say that there isn't something out of the ordinary going on here, something miraculous?

"I have one last item I want you to read. It is an account of an incident that happened on a US Army base involving a Jewish chaplain. Here," I said, handing David two sheets from my file, "please read this."

'The story begins on an army base in Berlin in 1974. Rabbi Wade, then a chaplain, befriended a Jewish American officer named Stuart. Stuart did not strike him as being a religious man and so Rabbi Wade was surprised one day to see Stuart wearing a yarmulke (skullcap). Upon questioning Stuart's reasons for donning this unconventional attire, Stuart told Rabbi Wade the fascinating story behind it. As part of their first year studies, cadets were enrolled in a course called History of Military Tactics & Field Strategies, taught by a three-star Lieutenant General with a Ph.D. in Military Strategy. The course surveyed the major battles in history, including those of the Ptolemies, Romans, and the Middle Ages, down to the latest battles of our modern era.

'During the final two weeks of the course, which were devoted to reviewing the material, Cadet Stuart raised his hand with a question.

"Why," asked Stuart, "did we not survey any of the battles fought by the Jews, either of ancient times (i.e. Roman-Jewish Wars) or of modern times (i.e. Arab-Israeli Wars)?"

"The normally friendly general snapped back with an order for me to see him in his office after class," remembered Stuart. Upon entering the general's office, Stuart was ordered to close and lock the door. "The general then told me that he would only answer my question in the privacy of his office," said Stuart.

"Do not think that the staff here at West Point has left the Jewish wars unnoticed," began the general, "we have examined and analyzed them and we do not teach them at West Point," he continued. "According to military strategy and textbook tactics, the Jews should have lost them. You should have been swept into the dustbin of history long ago, but you were not. You won those wars against all odds and against all military strategies and logic."

"This past year, we hired a new junior instructor. During a private staff meeting and discussion, the Arab-Israeli wars came under discussion. We puzzled at how you won those wars. Suddenly, this junior instructor chirped up and jokingly said, "Honorable gentlemen, it seems to be quite obvious how they are winning their wars: God is winning their wars!' Nobody laughed. The reason is, soldier, that it seems to be an unwritten rule around here at West Point that God is winning your wars, but God does not fit into military textbooks! You are dismissed," concluded the general.

"I left the general's office," continued Stuart. "I had never been so humiliated in my life. I felt about two inches tall. "Wouldn't you know it," I said to myself, "that I would have to come to West Point and find out how great my God is from a non practicing Presbyterian three-star general."

"I went back to my barracks," continued Stuart, "and dug down in my sock drawer to find that 'flap of cloth' that I threw on my head once a year. I said to myself: This thing is going on my head, because I found out, in essence, who I was and where I came from."

"David," I said, "these words, that 'God is fighting your wars' were said not by a Jew. They weren't uttered by a Rabbi. They weren't a quote from the Talmud. They were spoken by a three-star Presbyterian general!"

David sat there lost in thought for a while. Finally he said, "Rabbi, I see what you are driving at, it is clear that God is behind the scenes, that He is, in some mysterious way, orchestrating all that happens, but that makes the whole situation so strange. Why do it? You are telling me that He takes his people from country to country, and allows them to fall to the lowest abyss, to be tortured and murdered and only then does he save them. I don't claim to know much about God, but if He is that powerful, why can't He just let them live in peace? Why has there been so much senseless suffering, so much pain and torture. Rabbi, I don't mean to be argumentative, but I don't see how this helps me with belief, it just leaves me with more questions."

"David," I said, "it may take us awhile to get there, but I want you to understand that there is an answer to your question. An answer that is so right, so obviously true, that once you fully understand it, you will see that the question never really began. But, the answer isn't a one line, pat response. Rather, it is based on an outlook on life that is different from the one you now have. It is based on a different viewpoint on man, the Jewish Nation, our relationship with God, and most significantly on the very meaning of life. To fully understand that perspective will take some time; it won't happen in a few sessions. I hope over time that we will come away with a strong grasp of it."

Epilogue

Behold days are coming, says God, and I will send a famine into the land, not a famine for bread, nor a thirst for water, but rather to hear the word of God.

(Amos 8)

We live in truly wondrous times, times where we see progress of an unparalleled order: liberty, rights for men, comforts and conveniences, that even a generation ago were unheard of. We enjoy social progress, freedom from oppression, and an openness and tolerance that allows mankind to flourish. Technological improvements explode in front of us at a dazzling pace, each one outdoing the one before it. We also live in a generation that hungers, hungers for meaning, for purpose, for a reason behind it all. We live in a generation where there is an honest yearning for spiritual fulfillment. We, the Jewish people, were given the greatest, most fundamental system for spiritual enlightenment, we were given the Torah, the guidebook written by God Himself, as a beacon, as a light post, to guide us through our course in life, to help us find our path. More than something that adds to our life, it is the very focal point, the reason behind our lives.

We were given that Torah, written by God, as the ultimate spiritual guide, the work that will show us the path; answer our most fundamental questions, and show us the way. In it is all of the wisdom of the universe, because the One Who created the cosmos wrote it to serve that purpose. Our mission is to discover it, to seek it out. If we haven't had the life's opportunity to study it yet, then we need to find someone who can teach us, someone who is learned in its ways, who can guide us down its course, who can show us the wisdom of its path, and the truth of its ways.

The ways of the Torah are pleasant; so the journey, while it takes courage and fortitude is pleasant. In all my years of teaching Torah, I have never met anyone who said these ways are harsh. The only issue has been understanding its approach, and being open enough to listen.

We have this one opportunity, one shot, at this thing we call life. If we can wake up, and use it correctly, if we can find our path, then our life will be enriched for eternity, and our passage along the way will be pleasant.

If I have to give a purpose for this book, it would be as a clarion call, a call to my people to rediscover what we have known for generations. That, which was the bedrock of our people, and somehow in the fast paced environment of the times that we live in we have lost touch with. In our being thrown from shore to shore, exile to exile, we have lost touch with the basics, with that which has kept our people for these thousands of years. When we landed on these shores, and were thrown into the tempests of social and moral change, it seems that we lost hold of that eternal message. We now find ourselves as children and grandchildren of those who have lost their way. The route is there to return to our heritage; to return to that eternal tree of life.

And I will return the hearts of the fathers through the children,
and the hearts of the children through the fathers
(Malachi 3)